Diabolical Democracy Debunked

I0106271

By Gregory Heary

Systematically democracy in itself is directly opposed to religions, they cannot coexist. In both the Bible and Quran when Talut (Saul) was appointed to be the first king of Israel the people rejected God's decision and wanted to choose someone themselves, to which God said NO. This was one of the earliest attempts at democracy in the history of the world and it was divinely rejected as a form of government, because only God has the right to make laws and the laws of God are the only ones that can be just; since God is the most just and knows us better than we do ourselves.

Another attempt at democracy which had more effect happened with the pagan Greek Athenians who founded the Athenian League and created a proxy Thalassocratic empire. Inevitably they became obnoxiously corrupt and the inability of democracy to remove corruption from government was exposed, then their neighbors (allies) united against them and conquered them thereby ending the democracy experiment. Democracy has been subsequently retried again and again throughout history with similar results typically ending with the fall of an empire which historians incorrectly attribute to economic or military reasons, such as the Roman Republic, better known as the Roman Empire. In Italy before the renaissance democracy was tried again but the people rejected democracy and overthrew their democratic city-states replacing them with dictatorships. Notable examples include Perugia in 1389 CE, Bologna in 1401 CE, Siena in 1477 CE and Rome in both 1347 CE and 1922 CE. In fact, had democracy not been abolished in Italy the renaissance likely would have never occurred. The famous renaissance men like Leonardo Da Vinci, Michelangelo, Raphael, Donatello and such lived under dictatorships and as a result their talents were noticed and cultivated. Once democracy came to Italy again the talent disappeared and got lost in the masses because favoritism of talent contradicts democratic principles of equality, equal opportunity and equal rights. Throughout history people have tried democracy found out it sucks and doesn't work, but then later generations repeat the same experiments thinking they can make the impossible work for them when it's never worked before when even better people tried it. It's a misconception that democracy prevents dictatorship. Democracy and dictatorship are intimately related because every dictator has been appointed by a majority vote, which is the exact premise of democracy. Democracy doesn't promote peace within multi-ethnic societies, it promotes conflict pitting diverse groups against each other with genocidal foreshadowing as anyone living under democracy today recognizes even if they don't know those conflicts are caused by democracy. The philosopher Aristotle who lived under Athenian Democracy even said: "*Unlimited Democracy, is just like oligarchy, a tyranny spread over a large number of people.*" During the life of Aristotle, the definition of Democracy was: "*A State in which everything, even the law, depends on the multitude set up as a tyrant and governed by a few declamatory speakers.*"

Not one place in all of Colonial America contained a trace of democracy, the political structure was always that of a merchant state, or what is better known today as a corporatocracy. "*Natural rights*" and "*popular sovereignty*" were not philosophies promoted by anyone in American politics during the entire time period between 1607-1776 CE. Once a pseudo-democracy was established and the first tax levied, "*the people*" were completely taken by surprise and actually rebelled against the U.S. Government they had fought to create. One famous rebellion that gained too much publicity for history to ignore was the "*Whiskey Rebellion*" that was singularly raised in opposition to taxes. However, because these taxes were being paid to the U.S. Government and not the English Government, the founding fathers were on the side of taxation and mercilessly slaughtered the tax evaders they had previously paid to fight against the British in the American Continental Army. The tax rebels actually used the same slogan of "*no taxation without representation*" as a rallying cry saying that they weren't represented

and the taxation was unjust. This was because they thought political cliché *"the people"* meant them and that anyone who represented them would never agree to any taxation at all. Afterall if a politician really represents you then they wouldn't impose any taxes on you, would they? Unless of course there were people who wanted to pay taxes, but the American tax rebels were not such people and concluded they were not being represented and thus should rebel. Many were self-made pioneers who never had any help from Britain at all, they felt the Crown was simply extorting them without providing any benefit, inciting natives to harm them. When they fought in the revolution they believed *"no taxation without representation"* was a clever rhyme to say "no taxation" without giving their enemies a way to label them as anarchists. Regardless the U.S. government was not about to set a precedent of discussing taxation issues with its subjects, instead George Washington raised an army and the rebels were killed with bullets and cannon balls that were paid for with taxpayer dollars. Today they would loudly be called a "threat to national security" whereas in actuality they were just a threat to national taxation. To politicians a threat to taxation is a threat to their own financial security, so by considering themselves *"the nation"* they feel no qualms about calling threats to their own power, finances or reputation a "threat to national security" or *"the people"*. Regarding America, George Washington called it a "nascent empire", Thomas Jefferson called America an "extensive empire" and Alexander Hamilton referred to America as the "most interesting empire in the world". The alleged "reason" and rationality for US democracy deriving from intellectual thought was just a political placebo to get the philosophers to persuade the masses that the United States brand of democracy was somehow based on intelligent design so they'd view it as better than the false divine mandates claimed by the corrupt Christian European kings; even though rationality itself refutes democracy. America was formed during the "Age of reason" so reasonableness was cited as the reason for democracy despite democracy being unreasonable. Democracy was just the preferred way for the American aristocracy to break ties with the English crown and rule the masses themselves without causing the masses to view their mercantilistic state as an aristocracy. Those American anti-aristocratic patriots who found out they were scammed and fought back were met with federal violence. Ever since the massacre of the tax rebels, aside from a brief period during the civil war, the American citizenry has been forced to pay taxes against their will and are threatened with confiscation, imprisonment and death for "resisting arrest" if they don't. Some even quote Benjamin Franklin as having said: "'*In this world nothing can be said to be certain, except death and taxes*." not realizing he wrote that pro-tax pitch in 1789 CE two years AFTER signing the U.S. Constitution. During the revolution, before he got paid with American tax dollars, he was singing a different tune. If taxes were something as certain in this world as death, then early man would have experienced taxes just as early man experienced death. Adam and Eve never paid taxes to the government, neither did many other humans, even today there are modern advanced countries in the world outside of Euro-Merica that don't require citizens to pay any taxes at all. We don't have to be in paradise to live tax-free. The very fact that taxes can be evaded shows that taxes are not as certain as death. Yet the very same statesman who said that death is as certain as taxation also preached that there was to be absolutely "no taxation without representation". So in context doesn't that mean political representation is as certain as death? And that just as taxes are certain then so is representation? No, representation is not as certain as death? Well then I guess taxes aren't either and just as people do not have to have representation they do not have to pay taxes. While if there is to be no taxation without representation then I'll gladly keep my money and not be "represented" than be "represented" and have to pay taxes. To this day however the famous American democracy claims to be a "Representative Democracy" mainly due to that whole revolutionary slogan "no taxation without representation", hence their "Representative Democracy" is seen as a valid tax collector. The theory is that elected officials are representatives of "the people" so therefore "all the people" have to pay taxes. But if the one you vote for doesn't win, then realistically you aren't represented and that "representative" was forced upon you by the fixed election results. So if the one you voted for doesn't win then such voters should not have to suffer taxation since they truly don't have representation since their representative is not able to represent them in any political capacity not in theory nor in practice. (although in practice "representatives" who do win still don't really represent those who voted for them) Now some may say those voters' who voted for the loser "gambled their right to representation away and lost it in the election". That argument is invalid, but even if someone thinks it is, which if valid means elections take away the "right to representation" thus elections prove voters are not represented and "Representative Democracy" is impossible, what about those who don't vote? Why must the numerous non-voters pay taxes when they don't even "gamble their rights away by voting"? If voting for the winner means you have representation then both those who vote and lose as well as those who don't vote shouldn't have to pay any taxes at all. Truly if there is "no taxation without representation" then only those who voted for winners should pay taxes, but since its known elected politicians don't really represent those who voted for them even the voters should be able to be untaxed if they can prove their "elected representative" isn't really doing what they want. At the end of the revolution Americans got royally screwed. The popular slogan was "No taxation without representation" but most Americans are not represented yet they all gotta pay taxes through all possible orifices to their "elected slavemasters" in government offices. Taxes are a form of financial slavery and just as the American slaveholders convinced slaves they would die if they left the plantation, the American government has persuaded people that taxation is something that must be experienced, as certainly as death, and that somehow an election means unjust taxes become okay and legal. Historically a slave was simply a taxpayer, such as the Spartan slaves called Helots. Helots were allowed to live and work on their own land with the condition being that they'd pay a little less than 50% of their income to the Spartan government every year. Today we'd think that's just income taxes, yet back then people called it slavery. Whereas in Athens a "freeman" was someone who didn't work for anyone else, and was a citizen who voted on all Greek legislation and executive bills. Today we'd call that a politician, but back then such a person was a "freeman". Athenian freemen had slaves work for others on their behalf and every free Athenian citizen survived primarily off of employing their slaves to others and taking the income their slave earned along with tribute paid by foreigners overseas. So any taxpayer today who explained their life to a greek of ancient antiquity would be thought of as a slave, and ancient greeks would probably laugh because today's civilized taxpayers think they're "free". By ancient Greek standards freedom meant you kept 100% of what you earn, if you were not allowed to keep 100% of what you earn that meant somebody owned you. The same rule applied in the early Roman Republic, Plebians were the ones who paid taxes. The Patricians were "freemen" who governed, made laws, voted and didn't pay taxes. Plebians were a 2nd-class citizen not considered to be free because they paid taxes yet still got told they were citizens since they were technically not slaves of individuals since they only paid taxes to the state itself. Thus today most "freemen" are actually enslaved plebians according to Roman and Greek definitions of freedom.

Collectively as a species we're a bunch of idiots. Whereas democracy multiplies the stupid syndrome, thinking that if all the stupid humans combine together then the smart will somehow overpower the stupid by sheer numbers. Yet it doesn't take a genius to calculate that such math is flawed. Adding together stupid humans + stupid humans + stupid humans only gets you with more stupidity than you had with fewer humans. If you wanted to make humans have the dumbest political, economic and social policy possible, democracy is designed to discover and implement it. Although because of human arrogance and philosophers observing that corrupt people like Pharisees and Priests manufactured their own religions which Kings used to oppress people, the philosophers decided they would try to boost the human self-esteem and try their own hand at making a religion called reason, wherein ingenuity was to substitute God and they would be the initial prophets. Their plan worked but then to disguise their success, reason, equality, freedom, rights and liberty became the creed. Yet because it isn't an institutional faith few recognize it for what it is. The doctrine of human reason is a mythological fable. You can't reason your way into paradise. God didn't create humans and say "*just figure out everything on your own*". Adam pbuh didn't reason that a certain fruit was forbidden, he got told. Noah pbuh didn't reason he should build an ark. Abraham pbuh didn't reason his way to circumcision. Joseph pbuh didn't reason his way out of prison. Moses pbuh didn't reason his way to defeating Pharaoh's army and then reason up some laws to live by, such as the sabbath. David pbuh didn't reason his way into defeating Goliath. Jonah pbuh didn't reason himself out of the belly of a whale. Mary didn't reason herself into being pregnant with Jesus pbuh. If people think that human reasoning will lead them to paradise then that will be the reason they burn in hell. The true religion is reasonable but reason is not a true religion. There is a reason God sends prophets with miracles, because more than reason is needed to know who is right and wrong as well as how to live your life. Nobody thinks they could reason their way through school or work so why do they think they can reason their way through the test of life? To prove to an atheist the danger of human reasoning, ask them if they'd feel okay if their kid raised themselves without instructions from anyone or anything being raised solely by their own human reason?

Democracy is inherently anti-religious. Its still anti-religious even if it functions according to the theory that people select the rulers who make the laws. When the majority of people have the authority over the minority in deciding who makes the laws it is inevitable that the majority will oppress the minority. A majoritarian government in which the majority rules in all cases can never be a good or just government. The majority is not always correct, in fact history has demonstrated that the majority of the time the majority opinion has been wrong. Verily the majority of people are misled by Satan to a disastrous destination. So democracy is not designed to make the right decision, it is designed to make the popular decision. Any good idea to solve state problems will be controversial and unpopular. As such most governments cannot implement it, particularly if it's a democratic or republican style of state that needs the "support of the majority". Hence you will find governments who are popularly elected or reformed are always about at least 10 years late when adopting a new good idea. Such governments can never do what's right until the ignorant masses popularly agree that it is right, and usually by that time it's far too late and implementing that policy when the masses want it is rarely right and is actually wrong. This is because doing the right thing at the wrong time is in most cases wrong to do. Fools only agree to foolish ideas or they follow the crowd, or the money, or the charisma, or religion. Hence when the foolish masses agree, chances are that they only began to agree once the idea became foolish due to delay in implementation. This is the reason why democratic militaries don't exist, because indecision due to unpopularity threatens survival. Timing can make the difference between good and evil, and popular political acceptance delays action. Typically the most popular decision is the one that sounds the best but works the worst, which is why in democratic

countries when election time comes around even the politicians acknowledge that things in the country have been getting worse and worse. Unfortunately they blame the players rather than the game itself and people naively believe that *"this time it will be different, if only ____ is elected"*. They fail to recognize that is the exact campaign slogan of every candidate of all time.

There is no wonder why the morality in all democratic countries is declining when popularity is the most important factor when making up laws. Think about it, every law is passed based soley on whether it gets enough votes by politicians, not based on whether it is a good or bad law. The reason we have stupid laws is because the majority of people are stupid. In a "clean" election the smartest person in the world can walk into the booth to vote, then a mentally retarded person enters after them to vote, both their votes would hold the same importance. How can that possibly be an intelligent system? It's not. Democracy is a system of decision making whereby the loudest noise wins, not the smartest. To illustrate the stupidity of democracy as a form of government imagine if education was determined via democracy. What if students got to vote who their teacher was and voted what their teacher taught them and the majority vote determined the outcome? In such a system the stupid kids would get together and pick a bad teacher to teach bad, false or useless things with disastrous outcomes. Since academic curriculums aren't determined by democracy then how can our laws and leaders be determined by it? The schools that promote democracy refuse to implement it themselves. Democracy ensures that the right things don't happen and the wrong policies can continue to happen as long as enough idiots vote. Thus democracy cannot work or result in good in a world with idiots, stupidity, greed or basically any world with humans. In a democracy you can never "throw the bums out" because there is a practically unlimited supply who will fill the previous bums' chair. The Greek philosopher Plato aptly described how people live under a democracy: "[*The democratic youth*] *lives along day by day, gratifying the desire that occurs to him, at one time drinking and listening to the flute, at another downing water and reducing, now practicing gymnastic, and again idling and neglecting everything; and sometimes spending his time as though he were occupied with philosophy. Often he engages in politics and, jumping up, says and does whatever chances to come to him; and if he admires any soldiers, he turns in that direction; and if it's moneymakers, in that one, and there is neither order nor necessity in his life, but calling it sweet, free and blessed, he follows it throughout.*"

Despite having been pressured and registered to vote in high school, I choose not to. It is a false dilemma thinking you have to *"choose the lesser of two evils"* that statement alone is enough to prove that the democratic system has a satanic flavor. I have heard some people even call it demon-ocracy. Personally I'm not going to vote for evil of any degree, besides one vote does not make a statistical difference and isn't even noticeable. If 100 million people vote then the influence of your 1 vote is 0.000001%, which for all intents and purposes is zero influence. USSR ruler Josef Stalin revealed the truth about elections when he said, *"It's not who votes that counts. It's who counts the votes"*. What will I say on the day of judgment when God asks, *"Why did you vote for evil?"* One thing all politicians of democratic systems have in common is their immorality, they all agree on extorting money from people(taxing) in order to finance their goals. Voting just encourages them. No matter which candidate gets the most votes the government gets elected. If voting could actually change something you can be certain the government would make it illegal. Voters are not given the choice to vote on policies despite the internet and phone making that a possibility. Voters are forced to choose between dishonest candidates who they have no control over, should that candidate win they have no legal obligation to fulfill any of their campaign promises and there is nothing the voter can do about it. You actually have nothing to gain by voting and something to lose. You lose the time wasted voting and you lose the right to complain. When you know a game is rigged before you play, it's unreasonable to complain when you lose. All the political parties encourage voting because if there was ever a low number of voters the very legitimacy of the government would be called into question, at least internationally if not domestically. The primary reason the politicians are of lower and lower quality is because people will vote for anyone on the ballot thinking that if they don't the stupid masses will elect a bad candidate. If people said, "*we're not going to vote unless there is a decent intelligent honest individual as a candidate*" and followed through, a different class of politicians would emerge. Today it has become a frenzy that has led people to be comfortable with statements like "*voting for the lesser of two evils*" which is another sign that people know that voting is wrong and not the solution. Voting will not produce good results no matter who is elected. That is perhaps the best argument one can make against democracy, is that it involves voting for evil with no chance for a good leader coming from the results of an election; because no good person would want to rule according to such a system. If an oppressor gave you the choice to vote between having your left arm or your right arm being cut off would you choose or would you tell them they have no right to cut off either? If you choose then the oppressor would have become your servant following your orders and when confronted with the crime would only need to say, "*I only did what they voted for*" to get away without punishment. In a democratic country that might actually give them sufficient reason to be let go unpunished and leave you with one arm less, known as a fool rather than a victim. Sometimes the best action can be to not take any action. It is reported once a man was told he had to choose between 3 sinful options. 1. He could drink alcohol. 2. He could commit fornication. 3. He could kill someone. Facing these three options, all of which the man hated and detested, a devil whispered satanic logic and persuaded him to choose the lesser of 3 evils, so the man drank alcohol. As a result he got drunk and wanted to fornicate with a woman. The woman's son defended her, physically preventing the drunken man from fornicating. Out of rage the drunken man then killed the son and raped the woman. This resulted from the man voluntarily choosing to do evil even though he didn't have to, because of listening to deceptive satanic logic concerning a false dilemma. By voluntarily choosing the lesser evil it results in the most evil possible. The problem with political popularity contests (elections) is not the results, but the false beliefs that legalize such contests. In America the difference between Democrats and Republicans is that Democrats want America to be like the Greek Athenian League and Republicans want America to be like the Roman Republic. Both have a pagan plan for America, they just disagree which pagan plan they like better, thus America is Greco-Roman. Hence it Reeks of idiocy, corruption, injustice and oppression. America is and always has been a sinful oppressive immoral nation because it used a pagan blueprint for it's government. If one takes Greeks and Romans as role models you end up like them, and America has followed their footsteps; those footsteps eventually lead to a mighty fall into a deep dark pit. To vote is to support their journey taking more steps down the wrong road that does not lead to any type of paradise.

A politician with a limited number of terms is guaranteed not to care what the long term effects of their decisions will be. They're likely to be out of office by the time any bad outcome is realized which they are responsible for and probably won't even get blamed for it. If leaders know their job security depends on pleasing people they will not make the sacrifices necessary to ensure a better future. Politicians fear getting kicked out during the next election so they sacrifice the future in return for the present, as so many of us do in our own lives. The politician with a limited term is concerned with getting as much as they can out of their position before they lose it, so they don't care if the taxes are too high because it's their chance to get rich before being replaced. Not that a king is much better, but at least a king won't tax people into oblivion because a king wants to have something to collect the next time around and is more concerned about the future of the kingdom. Leaders with limited terms know that if they don't take it now then they won't have the chance to in the future, so they take as much as they can possibly get away with. The fact that before the person is even given power they are told they will have to leave soon, reveals that it is already known the person should not have that power or be in a leadership position to begin with. In any just system if the leader became incompetent, corrupt or unfit to lead then they would be replaced immediately, but in democracy they say *"well there is still X years left until the term is over"* so even after years of bad leadership and broken promises people are deluded into thinking they have to put up with continued bad service without the opportunity or chance for improvement. If politicians were treated according to their actions instead of their stated intentions they would be punished like bandits, murderers, thieves and the troublemakers who put obstacles in the road in order to hinder forward progress. No business or other relationship in society functions in this manner. Imagine if a sports team decided to keep a bad player as the starter on their team because his contract hadn't expired despite those on the bench being better players for that position. This is exactly what democracy does. If you were on a trip and realized the person giving you directions was leading you the wrong way, no one would continue following those instructions just because that's the one they started the trip with. If you are being led the wrong way in the opposite direction than you want to go, it's best to turn around immediately, because the further you keep going the longer it will take to get back to the right path if at all; you wouldn't wait until the next bathroom break to get directions from a different source. Why do we let these bad leaders finish their terms after their bad leadership has become evident? This is one flaw of democracy, it permits leaders who have been proven incompetent to maintain power which they are unable to use in the appropriate fashion, simply because they were elected by people in a wave of hysteria convinced of a pretense. You wouldn't keep using a vehicle that doesn't travel just because more payments are due. By keeping democratically elected leaders after they have revealed their inability is letting a mistake be perpetuated, in every other aspect of life we fix our mistakes and move on. At least in ancient Rome when they didn't like their politicians the pagan priests would make the years have less days in order for those politicians terms to end sooner and get them out of office. Roman consuls had short terms as well, the elections for Roman consuls were held every year and an individual could only serve once in their life. Meaning a Roman consul could only be consul for 1 year maximum in their whole life, yet still the Romans were so eager for bad consuls to be removed from office that they would collude to artificially shorten the calendar year throughout the empire just to get a few less days of X politician in office ruling them. Of course when it came to Senators Romans had them serve life-long terms, so it wasn't all short-term, but in Rome the political rules stipulated that elected leaders could only serve for 1 year maximum and non-elected leaders would serve for life. If Romans saw republics and democracies today with elected politicians who had terms longer than 1 year or multiple terms they'd denounce them as tyrants and be outraged the citizens allowed such fools to rule so long. Romans would insist that good politicians serve for life and politicians should either be given life-terms or minimalistic terms to limit the damage they can do. Romans realized that allowing politicians multiple terms of medium length was the worst possible way to have elected leaders rule them, since such frequent sizable terms allow time for politicians to be corrupt while removing the pressure for them to produce quick results or keep their campaign promises. Ultimately the practice of shortening a calendar year, in order to get rid of bad politicians who could only serve for 1 year maximum, was abolished by Julius Caesar when he created and ordained the Julian Calendar to be the standard preset calendar. Ironically the next year after he made the calendar years standardized, so that democratically elected politicians could serve their full term without being gyped by calendar manipulations, Caesar got assassinated by a mob of politically motivated people. So that's where not only have modern countries adopted the pagan Greek and Roman political models, they copied the crazy system of democracy and made it even worse than it was before. Seriously if you look at the ancient Greek and Roman democracies in depth, any objective person will say their governments were better than modern democracies are. Yet at the same time the objective person would see how their democracies were also unjust and flawed too. So maybe the problem isn't how democracies are run but with democracy itself? Regardless whether democratically elected or not, leaders should realize when they are no longer able to fulfill their duty and give up their power for the good of society rather than clinging to it for as long as possible. The duration of leadership should be based on performance not on a contract basis. Leadership is not something that should ever be put to a popular vote where elections are held requiring candidates for leadership to publicly campaign for votes. Why? Because you can't be leading a people and managing an organization if you are on a campaign trail trying to persuade people to vote for you. Any leader who neglects their duties to campaign for re-election proves they aren't fit to be leading, because if they were they would be doing their job instead of campaigning to get extra time to do the job they already have. Plus if one considers the money and time nation's spend on elections, those countries could end poverty if they just abolished elections and gave their campaigning money in charity. Any political party which "represents the poor" would be a poor party with meager funds because it's supporters are poor. Rich folk don't support the parties that support the poor. Yet no election can be "won" without lots and lots of funds. Thus democratic elections are only ever going to serve the aristocracy. Coincidentally it was the wealthy aristocracy that created the election system in America. People voting in elections doesn't fix countries nor will democratically elected leaders ever fix any real problems, the energies wasted by nations on elections are the primary reason those nations have so many problems. The elections are practically economic civil wars where all the money, time and energy is wasted for the sake of getting yet another unqualified bad leader. But that's why politicians like elections, because they know they aren't qualified to lead the nation to success and that the only way they could ever legally be in a position of governmental leadership is via an election process. Legally they can't get the job without the support of the mob. That's not to say elections are legitimate, but I'm just saying in theory if the votes were legitimate then elections are the quickest way to get unqualified leaders. The masses of most nations aren't even qualified to tell who is qualified. So elections are literally the unqualified masses voting for the unqualified and then they wonder why the election system hasn't been improving their nation. It's actually a good thing the votes aren't influential because if they were the results would be even worse. Although because the masses are led to believe their votes are influential then it makes them unqualified to recognize who is really in charge and thereby they are unable to change the true leadership of their nation if they felt oppressed enough to try to do so. Hence staged democratic elections are a fool's punishment, paradise and prison all at the same time. Sadly though voters tend to only view the elections as their salvation. However imagine if the impossible happened and a good leader was genuinely elected via democracy, what would happen at the end of the term? Is that not another indication that democracy is a broken system of nonsense? According to the law they would have to elect another and say: "*Even though this is the best leader we can possibly have, the rules are the rules and we have to take our chances and kick our good leader out hoping the new one isn't too bad. Good leadership was nice while it lasted, but you know we can't have good leaders sticking around because then the bad ones might stick around too. We must have constantly changing leadership, even though that's the most unstable type of leadership there is."* Seriously what if every few years you had different parents or a different body? Democracy is even worse than this because every day they are changing the rules making different laws. What kind of stability is there when something that was illegal yesterday is legal today and something that was lawful yesterday is unlawful today? This makes breaking the law have nothing to do with the deed, but is dependent on the time the deed took place. Two people can do the same exact thing at different times where one gets punished and one doesn't. That is not what I consider to be justice. In fact it seems more like it's "Just us getting oppressed by fickle fools who don't know what's right or wrong or when or why". Democracies neither establish nor legally enshrine fiefdoms of freedom they create unjust bureaucratic fooldoms.

There are only 4 tools Democracy has at its disposal:

1. Throw money at the problems hoping they go away and don't cause more problems.

2. Make new rules and regulations hoping they fix the problems caused by step 1 and hope that they don't cause more problems.

3. Set up and raise taxes to pay for new committees to supervise implementation of the new rules, regulations and agencies to fix the problems caused in steps 1-2 and hope they don't cause more problems.

4. Elect new people to do steps 1-3, since the previously elected people who did steps 1-3 caused more problems. Also hope the newly elected people fix everything and don't cause more problems. If this doesn't work then do step 4 again and again and again and again forever.

When we look at democracy for what it is we see that it is a faith, of which the central tenet is to hope that masses of idiots choosing which fool will rule them all doesn't cause more problems. Thus a belief in "Luck" serves democracies well. The main ritual of this faith is the election, during which people pray to the state hoping their problems will be solved. Everyone must submit to the decisions of the democratically elected government whether they elected them or not, whether they like it or not, whether it's right or wrong. There is no freedom, there is only the illusion of voter influence, with the continuous hope that the next election will solve the problems that have resulted from all the elections preceding it. Oh and on top of that the system is rigged too. This is because politicians determine and redetermine the voter districts. It's called gerrymandering and it means the government's politicians get to choose who can vote for each election. In practice if the government wants a certain party to win certain seats or positions they simply redraw the districts in any crazy shape they want in order to get the voters they want so that way the party they want to win will win, and the same goes for party primaries. Whereas the electoral college is how the American president is elected. Voters vote for X or Y but in reality their votes simply go to their state's representative and in theory they are supposed to vote for the majority but legally and in practice they vote for whoever they personally want to and the votes don't matter. Five examples thus far exist in U.S. history where the guy/girl who got the most votes running for president didn't win, in 1824, 1876, 1888, 2000 and 2016 CE. In the 1824 election Andrew Jackson had 38,00 more votes than John Quincy Adams and even had 99 electoral votes to Adams' 84, so by all accounts Jackson should have won, but John Quincy Adams was declared president simply because the House of Representatives said so. If their tricks still don't result the way the government wants then they just give different votes more or less value. The Americans just put up with it and say *"Democracy is the best. The USA is the best, because in other countries people can't vote."*

At the end of the day, the government picks the candidates, the government picks the voters, the government decides how much votes are worth and the government counts the votes and the government declares who the "winner" is. The government is in control of the entire voting process from start to finish. How then can voting change the very government which is controlling the voting process? The only way it can is if the government itself decides to change itself. But if the government is corrupt, how can a broken political machine fix itself? Democratic elections are literally just theatre. Elections are a government's way to say "X *is going to be in charge, but since you people don't like us or want us to pick who is in charge ruling over you we will put on a show so you think X was who the majority of people choose to be in charge. That way any complaints you have will be with your fellow taxpayers and not with us who really decided to put X in charge. This way you will never blame us, revolt or overthrow us because you will think the next elections can fix things."* The other reason elections exist is to make sure the politicians know that if they start thinking, saying or doing things the rulers don't want then they are easily expendable should they decide to deviate from the hidden leaders' path. Theologically democracy is a false religion and a pretty bad one made by pagans, except today it's even worse.

Every democracy if not disrupted always results in administrative absolutism in which people end up thinking the government is the solution to every problem and ask it for help and treat it as though its bureaucracy were God, with the elections being its primary religious ceremony. This is also known as statism which is a form of paganism in that the base is pure dogma where the individual is a servant to the mass idol created by man, intangible though it may be. The state is thus made by man in his own image. Statists believe their lives and wellbeing are privileges bestowed upon them by the State. They believe all that they do is and should be dependent and in accordance to the consent of the government whom they believe is the solution to all of their problems in life.

Yet how in the world could "government" solve the advanced problems of the people? If "the people" have no solution then where would the government learn the solution? Religion, animals or aliens are the only source of information the government can use that is not "the people". But "the people" don't have the solutions and think the government does which the politicians claim due to religion, except the politicians don't cite the source for their solutions. Statism is false because if we don't have or know the solution then the government doesn't either, since we all have the same availability of information. In reality behind the scenes most governments are the cause of most problems rather than the solution. It is by creating problems for people that the government ensures its "services" are in high demand. However the government presents data as cleverly as Satan does causing people to be deceived as to the situation they are living in, leading them to use poison as medicine again and again. Which is the same thing Satan does with sin, he makes us think the more we sin the happier we'll be despite sin being the cause of our initial misery. People are taught that laws of democratic governments are equal to laws from God, whether they are or not. Abraham Lincoln said, "*Let me not be understood as saying that there are no bad laws, nor that grievances may not arise for the redress of which no legal provisions have been made. I mean to say no such thing. But I do mean to say that although bad laws, if they exist, should be repealed as soon as possible, still, while they continue in force, for the sake of example they should be religiously observed.*" Lincoln was not alone in expressing this sentiment, most politicians believe this and even most political authority figures tend to attribute sacrosanct cult status to "the system" which they have authority over. The popular French statesman Maximilian Robespierre taught nearly the same exact thing as Lincoln, when he explained why democracies "always did the right thing", "*When the sovereign people exercise its power, we can only bow before it. In all it does is virtue and truth, and no excess, error or crime is possible.*" This is why most police have an attitude of superiority and loyalty to the law as though they were a holy warrior, because they are trained that all laws must be obeyed as though it is a religious obligation to obey man-made laws. This statismatic sentiment leads government employees/servants to truly believe that their government cannot commit a crime, especially when there is a threat to their government. As Robespierre said, "*If the revolutionary government must be more energetic in its actions and freer in its steps, does this mean that it is less just and less lawful? No! For it bases itself on the holiest of all laws-the good of the people; and on the most inalienable of all rights-necessity.*" Now you might be wondering what kind of job did Robespierre have before he was a politician? He was a lawyer who later became a judge but he quit his job as judge because he "*couldn't bear to sentence a person to death*". After he became a politician he sentenced many to death and made the guillotine famous. Being an "elected official" tends to change one's personality and moral principles. But the "Reign of Terror" was "for the good of the people", the 2nd most dangerous phrase a politician can ever say; the most dangerous is "for the good of the nation". Some think it's silly to think anyone is infallible but many of those same people view their government as infallible, or they act like it even if they don't think it. Most think as long as it's democratic it must be divinely guided. When people think Church and State are separate, the laws constitute religion. The separation of Church and State just means the state religion is not Christianity, it doesn't mean the State got out of the religion business. Governmental Laws were originally only religious. <u>Originally crime was defined as a sin that caused the wrath of the gods which needed to be punished by the community lest the gods destroy them due to the sin of the sinner/criminal. When civilizations developed all crimes used to be sins, but not all sins were punishable crimes. The religion dictated the laws of a country and punishing crime was a religious duty done by religious or political officials, which is why for many years most political officials were equated with being religious figures or even deities themselves.</u>

Thus democracy being the law of the people effectively makes the people their own lawmaker/god. Except since humans posing as gods were always doing so in order to commit oppression, democracy always causes spiritual/political oppression. Within democracies the "will of the people" is equated with the will of God. Democracies construct many collective tyrannies instead of an individual tyrant, unfortunately it's harder to overthrow collective tyrants. But don't take my word for it, the following are quotations from famous Americans concerning democracy:

"DEMOCRACY is nothing more than mob rule, where 51% of the people may take away the rights of the other 49%"-Thomas Jefferson, Drafter of the Declaration of Independence and 3rd president of the U.S.A.

"DEMOCRACY never lasts long. It soon wastes, exhausts, and murders itself. There is never a democracy that did not commit suicide." -John Adams, 2nd president of the U.S.A.

"When the people find that they can vote themselves money, that will herald the end of the republic."-Benjamin Franklin, famous statesmen and founding father of the U.S.A.

"No man's life, liberty, or property are safe while the legislature is in session" -Mark Twain, American Author

"Every election is sort of an advance auction sale of stolen goods." -H.L. Mencken, American Journalist and essayist

"Democracy is the theory that common people know what they want and deserve to get it good and hard." -H.L. Mencken, American Journalist and essayist

These Americans knew how dangerous democracy was, the thing is that America never fully practiced democracy. America was a mercantilist state based on mercantilism clothed in democracy. Mercantilism is bad enough and cannot even be moralized, which is why democracy was used as a costume for the American government. Yet the problem with wearing the mask of democracy is that most Americans don't know the government just used democracy as a mask for mercantilism and they start wanting to implement the monstrous system of democracy bit by bit until the mask will become the flesh. Currently America is an ideocracy, an ideocracy is a tyranny of certain ideas. In America these ideas are called "truths" and they say *We hold these truths to be self-evident*". Namely that God gave man a right to "Life, Liberty, the pursuit of happiness, and to rebel if they don't have the above 3 to their level of satisfaction." Although today the US schools don't teach that last "truth". Why? Because contrary to what the declaration of Independence claims, every government that ever existed or ever will exist, at all times restricted and contravened either the life, liberty or the pursuit which their subjects took to attain "happiness", some governments even restricted or contravened 2 or 3 of these things. So basically the ideal and allegedly just government advertised by the US Declaration of Independence has never existed and by definition can never exist, which therefore means the "self-evident truths" and God-given Americanist rights are false notions incompatible with reality, as even anarchy restricts/contravenes one's life/liberty/pursuit of happiness. Especially to attribute such "truths" or rights to God is disgraceful seeing how the government of David pbuh himself restricted the rights of life, liberty and the pursuit of happiness as did the government of Moses pbuh. Thus if these rights came from God all one would need to do is produce the God given law and documentation. Problem is that no such law or documentation exists, and cannot be conjured out of any religion which is why the drafters declared them to be "self-evident" because they had no other evidence or persons to support their claims aside from themselves. This is the rationalistic dream and it is ideologically idiotic. 1. To be self-evident means that the idea is known by everyone by themselves by default. It's even impossible to cite something that is self-evident because by citing it that would mean it's not self-evident. The self-evident truths are never spoken of or written about, by definition. 2. To say *"We hold these ideas/truths to be self-evident"* is an admission that they aren't truly self-evident because if they were then everyone would already hold them, not just "We". Also something that's self-evident doesn't need to be debated or proven by any evidence or justification whatsoever. So that "truths" need to be stated and labeled as "self-evident" indicates that they are definitely not self-evident and may not be truths as has been declared, in fact without any supporting evidence to prove these "truths" as true to simply label them as self-evident can only be done due to there being no legitimate proofs to support the alleged truths. The alleged truths have to be labeled as self-evident because there is no way to explain them without the "truths" being exposed as falsehoods. When the drafters of the US declaration of independence declared certain "truths" to be "self-evident", in legal terminology it means *"We believe X but we have no justifiable reason to believe it or persuade you to believe it, so we will just say everyone already believes it so people think if they don't already believe what we declare to be true they must be stupid and due to social fears of being the only one "not to get it on their own" they won't dispute our claims but will go adopt our unjustified beliefs without objection."* The very arguments the Americans claim support their rights are actually proofs that they don't have the rights they lay claim to. Fools think that this declaration guarantees or acquired rights for them but argumentatively the declaration eliminated the very possibility they could ever get such rights at any time by any means whatsoever. Alleged natural rights don't exist since rights come only from legitimate legislation promulgated by the authority of "nature". Whether one believes that authority is God or something else that is the only type of entity that can ever decree "natural rights". Otherwise if every species found in nature were to think up their own rights via reasoning then chaos would ensue because some animals would deem they have a right to eat other animals and those animals would deem they have a right not to be eaten and plants would get their "natural rights" trampled as animals ignored plant rights and the world would cease to function if any species could justifiable declare what "natural rights" it was entitled to. Basically "nature" would have to say what the rights are of every species in it's domain, and "human nature" is disqualified from declaring such natural rights because humans are not the originators or rulers of the domain of nature, we just live here temporarily. This type of ideological deception of allegedly self-evident entitlement, renamed as something other than entitlement, occurs whenever an ideocratic mentality spreads among a populace. Thereupon good arguments become unnecessary and the original complex good arguments are replaced by plausible simplifications or nothing. This gets done by charismatic leadership and charisma becomes the determining factor in political decision making. Yet charisma is simply emotionalism it has nothing to do with morality, good or evil, right or wrong. Both Moses pbuh and Hitler were charismatic leaders. Although when ideocratic states make leadership decisions based on charisma and disguise themselves as democracies it results in the perfect recipe for extremism. Semi-democratic Ideocracy is one of Satan's favorite types of governments because the people are trapped in it without any feasible way to get out and no matter how bad it gets the system is self-perpetuating because of the democratic guise and illusion of change. The only real change possible is the charisma levels and enthusiasm. The ideas are the governing force in an ideocracy however the right ideas are determined by the enthusiasm they generate, such ideas need not be right, reasonable nor rational and they don't even need to have the support of the majority. In such a state the loudest opinion which makes the most noise wins, regardless of what it is. This is evident in America today in that the majority don't like the policies of the government or it's actions, such a thing cannot occur in a democracy. It is literally impossible for the majority of the population to disagree with the leaders and the policies of a democracy, so America is not a democracy. By ideocracy hiding as democracy it becomes near unstoppable due to its reformers/enemies misidentification of it. The famous American ideocratic slogan of "self-evident truths" is a way of saying *"What we think is true and we don't have to prove it, but everyone has to agree with it because we say that they already do by default and we aren't wrong because they are truths, because we said so."* Hence it's no surprise that in the last 240 years America has been in more wars than any other country in the world. Of those 103 wars only 2 can possibly be considered to be a result of a foreign nation attacking America. Over 99% of the wars America has been involved in, America was the aggressor. The USA has been in so many wars, it's citizens don't even keep count If they did they wouldn't be able to use the standard American war narrative for every war they fight. What is the American war narrative? It goes something like: *"There we were living in perfect harmony and bliss due to our greatness, admirable work ethic and vastly superior political/moral principles and divine blessing/favor. Then without reason or warning we were treacherously attacked by barbaric evil cowards who hate us for our greatness/freedom/wealth and fight because they are evil/insane or jealous. Thus we must unite against evil and use extreme force to smash them so they learn to never mess with us again. Then those Barbarians will learn and thank us for the favor of crushing them so as to civilize them. We were innocent, never wanted 1 war and are God's favorite. This is why we are, always was and always will be the best nation ever. That is unless we stop being true Americans and lose the next war. Yet God won't let that happen because God blesses America because we are secular and let all believe and practice any/every faith."* All you have to do is replace the word "Barbarians" with a nation/ethnicity/faith or political group and that's the basic plot of every military war America has ever been in. Usually they add in a little sub-plot of liberating the foreigners from evil tyrants or uncivil/evil/immoral ideologies. Americans like to blame the leader of foreigners for their wars but if ever America were attacked for having an "evil leader" it's always the American people who are the victims never US leaders because Americans can never have evil tyrannical leaders that would be so bad as to justify a righteous foreign nation deposing them, because the brilliant Americans would vote them out of office and depose any evil leaders; or so the legend goes. Regardless of whether one believes the American war plots or not militarily speaking America is the most warlike nation in all of recorded history. On average the United States of America gets involved in a new war every 2.3 years. Why? This is because America is not a democracy but is an ideocracy that pretends to be a democracy.

 This brings up another point regarding states that claim to be democratic. Politically the Soviet Union was a democracy and held elections in which every adult citizen was allowed to vote. In 1917 CE Vladimir Lenin even introduced Universal Suffrage giving everyone in Russia the right to vote. In comparison America didn't officially grant universal suffrage to it's citizens until 1965 CE, but technically universal suffrage doesn't exist anywhere. For example kids and criminals still aren't allowed to vote. How then can one claim universal suffrage? This is because "universal suffrage" is defined as everyone who is capable can vote, with capability meaning "if the government says so". In the past skin color or gender was a factor that determined incapacity to vote simply because governments said it did. Some may not think universal suffrage or the definition of it is problematic but it's insane. For example why can't a newborn baby legally vote and have their vote count just as much as an adult's? People say that it would be unjust for babies to determine the affairs of the state when voting can result in consequences that effect other beings. Basically the babies would irresponsibly vote for their own interests and if babies got their way adults would get oppressed, therefore babies or kids are deemed incapable of voting not because they can't vote but because people deem kids having influence over their lives to be oppression. Yet why then are women allowed vote to effect the lives of men and vice versa or whites vote in elections with blacks or the rich vote alongside the poor. Won't the poor use their votes to oppress the rich? Won't the stupid use their votes to oppress the smart? Isn't that the reason why blacks wanted to vote, because the non-black voters were oppressing them? Isn't that why the poor and women wanted the right to vote so they could vote for revenge? The only reason people want to vote is to try to stop the other voters from oppressing them. How do X voters stop Y voters from oppressing them? It's simple, for X voters not to get oppressed by Y voters then the X voters have to oppress the Y voters and vice versa. The reason voting was restricted was in order to oppress without any risk of reprisals. Voting is the opportunity to manipulate the law in your own favor. Voting is only valuable when it is a tool of political favoritism and oppression. If voting can't be used for oppression or favoritism then it is pointless and nobody would ever vote. It is only when the law or government can be used for injustice that people want to have political power and influence. Thus if some can vote then they will oppress the others who can't, and if everyone can vote then it will be to defend themselves from oppression by causing injustice and oppression to others who lose in the voting process. Hence since votes can be a tool of oppression if they can influence society then nobody should be allowed to vote in order to prevent any and all types of oppression. Yet in most democracies today most people are allowed to vote. Why is this? Because the votes don't matter or result in the voters influencing their government. If they did then voting would always result in oppressive incompetent unjust governments. Which doesn't mean that just because votes don't matter the governments aren't oppressive, they can be and most are. What it means is that if people are voting there are only 2 results. If the votes count then oppression will occur, if the votes don't count then for voting to take place when it doesn't count is a sign of oppression to such a severe amount that theatrical voting is a necessary political ploy the state must use to avoid revolution. Thus whether votes count or not the occurrence of the democratic ritual of voting is a clear sign that oppression is taking place. The number of categories who are restricted and prevented from voting approximately indicates how oppressive the government is. The more categories of people there are who can vote the more oppressive the government is. I repeat that the more who can vote in a country's elections the more oppression there is, either because the votes count and the majority oppresses the minorities or because the votes don't count but a big show is put on to prevent the population from realizing they have no ability allotted to them by their government to stop the oppression. To prove this point women in Communist Russia were allowed to vote three years before women were allowed to vote in America. The Soviet Union in accordance with their economic communism believed and preached that all it's citizens were equal. So does this mean 1917 Russia was less oppressive than 1965 America? Russia in 1917 CE under Lenin was more democratic than America was under Wilson. Yet Americans had such enmity for the Soviet Union they labeled it an enemy of democracy despite the Soviet Union actually doing democracy better and more fully than America did. Today North Korea(known as the Democratic People's Republic of Korea) is also a democracy which holds elections in which every citizen over the age of 17 can vote in. Meaning citizens can vote in North Korea at an earlier age than they can vote in America. China and Russia are also democracies. Yet most Americans don't consider any of these countries to be democracies. Why not? Because they don't do things the American way, however on a technical political level they are democracies. People will say that the elections are fixed in those countries and only people the governments' want to win are allowed to win, but that's exactly what happens in America too. The only difference is that the American government has had many more years to practice being a corrupt fake democracy so they put on a much better show to fool more people than the other countries are capable of. So much of American politics are planned that it's disgusting. What's worse is the politicians confess from time to time and people still ignore their confessions that the political issues and actions are planned well in advance. Hence 4-time US president Franklin Roosevelt said, "*Nothing happens in politics by accident, if it happens, it was planned that way*". Another thing which president Franklin Roosevelt said about politics was that "*Presidents aren't elected, they're selected.*" So when US voters claim presidents get elected, tell them that the man who has been US president 4 times says they are not elected. Who do you think knows more about the matter of becoming president, the guy who was the actual US president 4 times or some American voter?

The more scandalous a president is the more controllable they are and since I was born in 1992 there hasn't been a president elected in any country who hasn't been immoral to a scandalous extent. Currently in America, my birth nation, as I write the top two candidates of both parties for the next presidential election are both under criminal investigation for crimes yet americans think regardless of which criminal wins they have the best governing system ever known to mankind. Many citizens are incapable of political foresight since it involves extensive economic, historical, cultural, sociological, psychological, political and religious knowledge, and even then political prediction is speculative with innumerable variables. The point is most citizens are oblivious to the fact that their government's have planned policies decades in advance, including the types of leaders they will have, with most governments having plans for future policies/wars/changes centuries in advance. <u>In reality power has never been put to a vote in any country throughout all of history.</u> The only difference with Americans is they pretend their elections are different because they get told they are, but when China, Russia or North Korea says the same thing then Americans don't give them the same benefit of the doubt. In reality they aren't democracies and people are right to say they aren't, but not one country in the world today really is, so people are wrong to claim that any government in the world is a democracy. The ancient pre-colonized Native Americans were more democratic than the countries of today and that's what's really funny about America in particular. The land of America was a lot more democratic before the whites "introduced democracy". Truly it's a joke to claim the colonists established democracy when the Native Americans were more democratic than the US Americans have ever been. America actually became far less democratic when the United States came into being. The United States of America has always been less democratic than the "savages". Most nations today are ideocracies following America's example pretending to be democracies, so it's more appropriate to call them decoyocracies or say that they are mockingdecrazies. Today in America there are no true democrats, republicans, libertarians, socialists, independents or any other of these "political parties"; all of the politicians are really decoyocrats serving the American ideocracy. Either they're decoyocrats or very confidant idiots. Kingship wasn't really replaced by democracy it was just disguised and controlled. Before the reimplementation of the pagan political faith of pseudo-democracy leadership in many countries was heavily influenced by birth as political succession was lineal or lateral. However when the next generation of leadership is determined by birth this makes it difficult to have long-term government planning and causes instability in case of loser descendants who are disastrous leaders or situations where no heirs to the throne cause political turmoil. Thus democracy and elections eliminated the instability, fragility and unreliability of dynastic succession. Now instead of government leaders being set since birth with the administration hoping their destined King to be does what they planned for, they can simply use elections to ensure the leaders always follow the plan the political elite, foreign puppeteers or aristocrats have set for the nation. Hence democracies are actually easier for the ruling class to control over time than a kingdom is, while the citizens of a nation actually have more influence over the government if their ruler is not elected than if he is. A King can always be persuaded by the people, and if the King can't be then the next one can be or the heirs can be influenced. Yet under the democratic decoy governments popular amongst people today, people not only can't influence their "elected politicians" but if they do manage to change their politicians then the puppetmasters just use the elections to get new ones. Democracy actually takes power away from the people, yet due to political ignorance they think democracy empowers them. If you want to know what democracy is really like in practice then research the French Revolution of 1787-1799 CE. It is also known as the "Reign of Terror". During which the French abolished the Crown, abolished the aristocracy, abolished the Church, abolished the merchant class and abolished nearly everything that was undemocratic. Sounds like freedom right? All those groups who "control us" were abolished. The French took America's lipservice about freedom, equality and democracy and put it into full practice only to realize it wasn't quite what they thought it would be. During this time in France the elected politicians tried to "equalize property" and divide the wealth of the nation equally among every single citizen so there was no such thing as economic classes, since equality meant that every French citizen legally had to have exactly the same amount of money in their pocket as every other French citizen. Democratic France tried to abolish profit because for someone to gain profits meant there was an inequality in the citizens' financial situations. Profit was deemed evil because to profit means to be unequal, and people gaining unequal profit could/would lead to people having unequal power, financially speaking but also politically speaking since money can make elections turn out favorably for those with more finances. In Democratic France every single person was given the right to be hired, however to keep everything equal nobody was allowed to have any advantages irregardless of their skills or expertise. There was one standard wage, if you were a French citizen you got paid the French wage. Nobody had to worry about being rich or poor because everybody was paid exactly the same amount no matter what job they did, irregardless of who they worked for or how long they worked. You see for everyone to be truly equal they had to earn the same amount but obviously everyone couldn't work the same amount of time due to practical reasons and due to working different jobs. To solve this dilemma workers got paid a daily wage whether they worked 1 hour or 24 in a day. As the saying goes "a day's worth of wages for a day's worth of work", this means one person's daily output of productivity equals everyone else's because they are equal since "everyone is equal"(which is "so true it is "self-evident""). Some may misunderstand this as welfare but it wasn't because everyone worked by definition and as equals they had to be paid equally to be fair because otherwise if merit/skill/productivity/time/effort/need/demand were to determine monetary remuneration then people would be unequal and treated unequally. The French thought treating people unequally was oppressive/illegal because they believed everyone was equal and deserved equal treatment. Yet not only was equality implemented amongst the quantity of money but every man was to live in the same type of house and have a wife and have children. While to be fair, divorce was made to be as easy to do as getting married, and to keep everyone equal no distinction was to be made between legitimate and illegitimate children. Fornication and adultery were made legal because to prohibit such sexual sins would mean to make certain people unequal to others which could lead to unequal treatment. This is because for a wife to be treated differently than any other girl amounts to unequal treatment. The same applied to family, family ties in New France could not unequitably determine treatment. French people were legally expected to treat everyone as though they were family, no favoritism for family relations was allowed because to treat blood relatives better than strangers is to consider people unequal which was wrong and to treat people unequally was a crime and "obviously barbaric". For someone to view/treat their mother/wife/daughter/aunt/sister any different than they would a unknown prostitute was unequal and considered uncivilized since "believing everyone is equal and deserves to be treated equal = enlightenment". The French thought if only everyone was treated equally then everyone would be happy and nobody would suffer at all. Some may disagree with this doctrine but that's equality and even if one still disagrees they aren't allowed to think their opinion is better and another opinion inferior because to think some doctrines/policies/ideas are better than others is to not believe in the equality of ideas. And what kind of "civil folk" thinks ideas aren't all equal or that all people aren't equal or that they "deserve (have a right) to be treated equally"? The French Convention also deemed that gold money would be replaced by paper money which they called assignats. The calendar was remade to have 30 days in every month and 10 days in every week, the months were given different names and the days were simply called "first day, second day, third day...." etc. Some even suggested abolishing all religion because it became obvious that every religion known to man spread the idea of inequality and unequal treatment of people due to religious differences, so some said Reason should replace God. Although it was determined that Atheism and Reason also spread inequality because they were inherently aristocratic. This was when many French people started to deduce that reasoning seemed to imply the doctrine of all people being equal might be unreasonable. So therefore for everyone to be equal "reason" was deemed to be a criminal or heretical doctrine. So instead of atheism or reason becoming the state religion as had been planned by the rationalists and pro-freedom pro-democracy pro-equality movement, a "Supreme Being" or "Eternal Being" was acknowledged but no details were given about this being because to do so may create inequality. For everyone to be equal everyone had to know absolutely nothing at all about the "Supreme Being" that existed. Likewise nobody could try to worship this "Supreme Being" that existed because then it would cause inequality since some might worship it better than others or for longer than others. Eventually when the democratic pro-equality abolishers decided to rule, the democratic populace abolished the abolishers because they violated the principles of democracy and equality as well. Since if everyone is equal then nobody can ever truly be in charge, to have a leader would mean they are not equal to everyone else. Thus the executioners of those who opposed democracy and the doctrine of equality which it taught were also executed because by executing people the executioners became unequal to all others. In reality equality became the French religion and they tended to kill anyone who dared to suggest it's impossible to have a world built upon the doctrine of everyone being equal. They believed in democracy and equality despite nature being both anti-equality and anti-democratic with inequality being a crucial necessity for civilizations to progress. Right or Wrong (both being equal) Equality became the religious faith of New France and the French army set out to violently convert the world to its gospel of "Equality, Liberty and Fraternity" rescuing everyone from tyranny and eradicating inequality. Some French people even went so far as to declare that the revolutionary leader Robespierre was "*the Messiah whom the Eternal Being had promised to reform the world.*" Eventually France became so chaotic, or democratic, that Napoleon Bonaparte was put in charge to keep the peace of those who wanted to kill those guilty of being unequal/superior or promoting inequality. Then Napoleon was defeated in the middle east when trying to conquer Syria and the French army was lost, but since the news traveled so slowly when Napoleon came back to France they thought he was victorious and made him a hero. Next Napoleon lost in Russia and was exiled, he returned from exile was remade emperor and then got defeated by the English. So Napoleon decided he would come to the United States, probably to get elected as Emperor of America; since he sold about 13 states of territory to America for $15 million. However the English captured him before he could finish the full voyage to America. From 1815-1848 CE France returned to monarchy. Thereupon France returned to democracy in February 1848 CE and ended up abolishing slavery in April, 1848 CE. In December, 1848 CE France elected Louis-Napoleon Bonaparte to be their president by a vote of 5,500,000 out of 8,000,000. In 1852 CE Louis-Napoleon became Napoleon III, the Emperor of France by a vote of 7,500,000 out of 8,000,000. He went on to rule for 18 years before being captured by foreign enemies in battle. So democracy in France didn't just result in an emperor once, or twice, but three times in 50 years democracy resulted in elected French leaders who became emperors. Its almost as though "emperor" is just one of the things a democratically elected leader is. Yet theoretically and in practice during that time France was technically the perfect democracy, it fully followed the theory of democracy even better than communists followed communism. This is why no famous "thinkers" of the 19th century ever supported democracy, for centuries the "geniuses" have said democracy is crazy. The lesson is that democracy is bad, whether it's practiced fully or partially and will always lead to despotism, either directly or indirectly. I mention this because when many Americans find out America isn't a democracy they think democracy is the solution because of their ideocratic American upraising or ideology. But democracy is not the cure, it's just another disease. Just ask the British colonists of the 1700s CE how Parliamentarian democracy worked for them. Yes that is something many forget, in that America did not reintroduce the world to ancient pagan democracy, Colonial Britain was already practicing democracy and was operating under a parliamentarian-monarchy much like they are today. The "Americans" revolted against the British because they hated living under British democracy. When America exported it's version of democracy mixed with freemason religion, the French "*Reign of Terror*" happened followed by the Napoleonic wars, ever since the US has exported an ideocratic doctrine of Americanism but called it democracy instead. In truth what's called the "American Revolution" was the 1st British Revolution in the Americas, whereas the true American Revolutions such as the early American anti-tax rebellions in the 1700s CE and the American Civil War in the 1860s CE were swiftly defeated. Americans lost their revolutions so they and their historians incorrectly claim the colonial British revolution to be theirs. The early American revolutionaries had a fighting chance and lost, but today no violent revolution in America would win unless God helped them, a lot. Americans know this so most of them pretend they aren't subjected. Americans are much like how Romans were in the Roman Empire, and there was no Roman revolution. Historically the Roman empire fractured with the western empire becoming the many states of modern Europe and the eastern Byzantine Empire being liberated via Islamic conquest.

Even "write-in" candidates are sinful because such "write-ins" legitimize the system and secondly the "write-in" actually gets counted as a free vote for whoever the vote counter, if there was one, decides. The vote counter can just say *"To me that handwriting looks like it says X candidate."* and nobody ever bothers to check to see if who they intended to vote for was actually who the government said they voted for. Honestly voters are so stupid they actually think the government is not corrupt enough to say they voted for X when in reality they voted for Y. Seriously the citizen voters never check to see if their vote was counted accurately because they just have blind faith in democracy. Also people think that a "write-in" candidate means you can write in a vote for whoever you want, but that's not how it works. A voter can only vote for a registered government approved candidate. A write-in vote only counts if it's for a registered candidate the government approved of but just didn't put on the ballot because they weren't one of the government's top choices for mascot. You see that's the other thing about elections, in that you have to register as a candidate with the government and if the government doesn't want someone to be the leader they just reject their application because they can, because they are the government which makes the rules. So literally all this talk about "the government doesn't want X to get elected, because they'll fix it all and end the corruption" is pure lies. If the government really didn't want somebody to get elected they would just reject their application to participate in an election and nobody would ever be told they were a "possible option". Only people the government wants to be their mascot can ever participate as a candidate in the election. The government chooses who is eligible for office, those who aren't with the government's program never get approved as an eligible candidate. To be a candidate means to believe and agree with what the government bureaucracy wants. No politician can even get on the ballot to get a vote unless they are approved by the government and the government wants them on the ballot to get a vote. Thus you can only ever vote for who the government wants you to vote for because those are the only ones who can be voted for. Basically elections are a way for citizens to pick a mascot who is just a public face for the government without any true power. Citizens if their votes even count for anything, it would only be a matter of whether they wanted a mascot who was male or female, black or white, blue, brown or green eyes, hair color, young or old, fat or skinny, rich or less rich, dumb or dumb, dishonest or dishonest, immoral or immoral and finally evil or evil. Yet at the end of the election the government's choice gets the job no matter what and the policies the government planned to implement get implemented and if people don't like what their government does they just blow off their steam on the mascot thinking it's the mascot's fault for what the government is doing; because the mascot, media and government said it was. Truly elections are the biggest type of fraud by which a institution can control it's people while making their subjects think they aren't really in total control. Democracy is slavery with the illusion of choice/freedom/equality so that the slaves are happy to be slaves and love to be oppressed/exploited. The extreme stupidity of voters is proof enough that voting should never be used as a method to decide anything important. If you ever want something done right, don't put it to a vote.

A government must be corrupt to allow voting, being a democracy just means they are so corrupt they try to hide it. The votes are purely political theater done for religious reasons to make the faithful "feel good" about doing something under the illusion that their voice is heard and can influence the one that has a gun to their head requiring them to pay taxes, but in reality they are doing less than nothing to change things. Many Americans actually think the ones with the guns telling them where to vote, when to vote, who to vote for, how much their votes are worth and who "counts the votes" will actually let them tell the government what to do and the government will do it because of voting. The government controls every aspect of the election but the citizens think voting is some type of loophole that will cause them to control and change the government, because the government told them it was. The government lies to the citizens every day of the week and they know this, but then when a ballot can be used they think *"Well the government promised they'd do what we want if we pick who they allow us to pick."* They foolishly religiously believe that the government who they know lies to them about nearly everything, even the weather, is telling the truth when it says *"Your votes control us, we promise."* Honest people know that in general the politicians are liars and lie about most things they say, yet the one thing all politicians unanimously agree upon is that *"Voters control the government."* Isn't it suspicious that the 1 thing professional liars agree upon is their unproven claim that voting can influence the government? They lie about almost everything but when they all agree we are supposed to believe them? Are they more likely to unanimously lie to us or unanimously tell the truth? In 1957 CE the Senator of Nevada George Malone, commented: *"I believe that if the people of this nation fully understood what Congress has done to them over the last 49 years, they would move on Washington; they would not wait for an election."* People have fallen prey to the school book myths about these historical politicians who in reality were little different than the ones we have today. Even the politicians of today are worshiped and famous celebrities make statements equating the political leaders to be godlike. I'm purposely not citing their names to avoid giving these celebrities any more attention than they already have. May God help us to see politicians for what they really are. Don't let them simply having lived in the past make your opinion change, treat them for who they really were not who people think, claim or would like them to be. As an example in regards to religion the popular US president Abraham Lincoln said, "*When I do good, I feel good. When I do bad, I feel bad. And that is my religion.*" and "*Neither Heaven nor Hell. It is simply Purgatory.*" Meaning Lincoln viewed himself as his own religious guide and needed no instructions via revelation or a prophet and Abraham Lincoln didn't believe in Heaven or Hell. Regarding drunks and alcoholics Abraham Lincoln said, "*I believe, if we take habitual drunkards as a class, their heads and their hearts will bear an advantageous comparison with those of any other class. There seems ever to have been a proneness in the brilliant and warm-blooded to fall into this vice.*" Such statements are proof enough that Lincoln was an irreligious idiotic immoral imbecile. By giving such bad people in the past our respect it makes us have lower standards in the present and get stuck with worse leaders. An important point is that bad governing is systematic, a bad government is never the fault of "*just X president*". If say for example the US government were in theory bad, then they've been bad for a long time and their incompetence or evil cannot be attributed to just 1, 2 or 3 presidents but a legion of bad governing for many years. Many people fall for the election campaigners' trap of thinking it's all X president's fault so then they vote thinking the next one can fix everything just as they've been promised by every candidate ever. While I can refute that notion, since I've never been president some might not believe me when I say no president can be bad enough to screw up a country, especially in a democracy because a democracy is designed theoretically to prevent such disasters. To prove this I will cite Abraham Lincoln who despite his moral/religious flaws taught exactly what I just wrote when he said, " *While the people retain their virtue, and vigilance, no administration, by any extreme of wickedness or folly, can very seriously injure the government, in the short space of four years.*" So for any people who blame X president for ruining their country, that can only happen according to Lincoln if the people themselves have no virtue and vigilance. Thus since people tend to believe they are virtuous and vigilant the only way a government can be bad is if it has had a long chain of bad leaders. Regarding America I think they've had bad leaders since 1776 CE, and when you have 240+ years of bad leaders, the next one is probably not going to be able to quickly fix a mess that took so long to make. At least such a mess can't be fixed via democracy. Yet while we may not be able to right the wrongs of modern politicians we can correct the memory we have of past politicians and prevent the idolization of irreligious inept ignoramuses. We can fix the memory of the bad leaders in the past by rejecting the romantic political myths we get told about politicians in the past being heroes instead of politicians. The politicians of the past were little different than those today and the people never thought their wicked politicians would become heroes, get statues or get holidays either. For us in the present or future to idolize such people gives us no benefit and insults those who do deserve to be remembered with honor, such as prophets. I'm not saying to pick a bone with dead people but don't polish the memories of bad people, because then after the corpses of the corrupt corrode they could become an idol. You can't throw the present bums out if you can't even spot the bums of the past. Democracy and history has given us a "Bum Standard", most national heroes were villains in their own time and by idolizing them we get stuck with villainous leaders today. We frequently view or treat God's prophets like they were bums and we view/treat the bums like they were prophets.

In regards to the theory of democracy it has never been implemented yet, what most people believe to be democracy is actually "national democracy" I use the term "national democracy" because in theory the faith of democracy is the "rule of the masses" which means it's a global system and to restrict the majority vote to members of your own nation is not true democracy. If the majority vote is always right then the majority of people in the world should vote on everything, because to only have your nation vote would not constitute a majority and thus such voters will, according to democratic beliefs, be wrong every single time. That's the hypocrisy of those preaching national democracy, in reality they are promoting anti-democracy where a majority vote of a minority decides things. Most don't promote global/true democracy because they are nationalists who don't really believe in democratic principles but just think their national majority should be able to decide things for their nation, because their nationalism dictates all other nationalities are inferior or unqualified or untrustworthy. Yet if people of other nations are untrustworthy, then who is to say people of other states or cities aren't? What about the government? Are they trustworthy? If not then why do politicians get a vote? Seriously people are afraid of foreign voters but they aren't afraid of their own blatantly corrupt politicians voting? With most governments today a foreigner desires better things for your nation than the native politician. Democracy can only be a global faith/system while national democracy is the hypocritical political exigency, which most think is "democracy" because they are really ideocractic nationalists playing games. No democratic nation in the world today wants a global democracy due to their nationalism, even though if democracy were fundamentally a correct system then a global democracy would be best. Ultimately if the religion of democracy is believed in, preached and practiced, it leads to a global system/faith that has everyone in the world ruled by 1 government in which everyone allegedly has their vote count. However if there is only 1 government that rules the whole world, do you really think they are going to count the votes? Yet that's what democracy leads to, a global government where everyone in the world can influence everyone in the world via votes, in theory. However even in theory if it weren't corrupt, such a global democracy is crazy. National democracy is no less crazy in theory nor practice but people believe it because it's a religion and not just a legal system. However those who do actually believe in democracy believe everyone should believe in and practice it, without realizing the reason they believe that is because to believe in democracy means one must believe in a global democracy, at least subconsciously. Democracy is all or nothing, either everybody votes as a world or nobody is really practicing it. Hence democracy is spread by military violence or money if propaganda doesn't work. At this time few are calling for global democracy and "national democracy" is just a myth preached by ideocracies.

There is only one way to stop an injustice, it should be obvious what it is but for some reason it has become a secret. No matter what injustice it is, the only way for one to stop an injustice is to......... stop the injustice. A person cannot destroy the prison system by getting sent to prison and becoming a prisoner or by being a prison guard. Likewise joining the "bad guys" will only make you into a bad guy too. A bad system cannot be reformed, the only hope is to reform ourselves and for the people that are part of that bad system to reform themselves and abandon/abolish it. Personally I even know people who thought they could fix a bad system and got elected to be presidents of said associations. One of them I even talked to before they got elected, we both agreed the current president of the association was a problem, but I said the problem is the democratic system that elected the problematic president so by you becoming president you can't fix it as you think because even if you did then when the next president takes your place they will change it right back, unless of course you abolished elections and the system itself. They disagreed and got elected as president. About 7 months later I overheard them ardently complaining to their advisors about how they can't change anything, can't rely on people to do simple tasks, can barely do anything because of internal politics, were disgusted with the whole association and just planned to finish their term trying to keep the association united as one. I didn't say "I told you so" but every single elected leader of every single organization has this same problem, except some just like the position and pride that come from the title so they desire it longer than others. So I don't care what organization or system it is, if it has fundamental flaws or is corrupted then joining it will not fix it. No system is designed to destroy itself, yet that's what people think they'll make it do by utilizing a bad system. It doesn't work, that's what Satan wants people to do. Satan wants people to be his friend thinking they can change him and they are the ones who end up getting changed by Satan; every single time. If you hate a satanic or bad system as you should, and you join that system trying to change it, then by joining that system and being a part of it you must hate yourself too. Thus if you join a bad system or group, you will either end up hating yourself or changing your attitude about the system or group. You'd be surprised how often the system changes those who joined it with the intention of changing it. The people change, the systems don't. So to change the system the people must change and collectively starve the system. I repeat nobody can "change the system". Many people think they are different or that X system is different and can be changed for the better, this can't be done. To illustrate how impossible it is to change a bad system one can examine criminal gangs. Now what if somebody told you, "*I'm going to join a criminal gang in order to gain influence over them and/or become the leader of the gang. Once I have influence over the gang or if I'm the leader of the gang then I'll be able to change the gang and get them to stop doing crimes.*" Everyone would agree such a person is crazy and will fail. There are only 3 ways to fix a fundamentally flawed system. Either you kill all the members, imprison all the members or they all quit and abolish the system themselves. Option 1 is not feasible, nor safe, nor wise, nor desireable plus its extremely sinful. Option 2 is illogical and impractical and extremely sinful. Option 3 is unlikely but possible. However the point is that joining a bad organization built on flawed principles never purifies it. So I don't care whether it's a peaceful democratic society or a violent criminal gang, you don't fix it by joining them. They have to quit the system and join you not the other way around. One doesn't get influence over others by joining them, that's how they get influence over you. These are basic political facts that few understand. A change in membership quality or quantity does nothing to improve a system built on a flawed foundation. The premise and principles of the organization/system must be fixed at the fundamental level with a new foundation and organization/system being born in order to replace the broken system. Basically when political systems or organizations are broken, you can't fix them without rebuilding from scratch. The worst flaw of broken and/or flawed systems is that they give people the false impression that they can be fixed. Wherever there is a bad organization there are bad principles and ideas at the root of the problem. The systems are built on ideas, when you change your ideas your ideas don't change, you just replaced your old ideas with new ideas. Thus systems can only be replaced they can never change, those who try to change them get changed themselves. Everyone who has ever become a member of a bad system or organization did so with the intentions of improving it and they failed. So the key to success in fixing the system is to not join in it but create an alternative system. It's best to have God in your group than abandon God and join another group intending to fix it for the sake of God.

The saying should not be "*Only God can judge me*" but rather "**Only the law of God is valid to judge by**". According to the biblical Jesus pbuh, only the laws of God have legitimacy. Therefore if someone is judging you based on how much you follow the laws of God, you have no right to complain, it is the only standard you should be judged by. The catchphrase "Only God can Judge" is supposed to mean that, "*Only God can judge what's right or wrong, whereas God has done that and the prophets taught us how to judge stuff. Therefore any other standard of judgement whether personal, civil or criminal is invalid because only God can judge and we have his judgements. Thus your judgement is rejected and replaced by God's judgement, in this life regarding all matters and the next life.*" That is what "Only God can Judge" used to mean, but then future generations forgot the fundamental doctrine but kept the short catchphrase and developed a Satanic doctrine where they reject God's judgement because it comes to them from people and instead use their own judgement; or some other standard of judgment that is not God's. To say "Only God can Judge" is to say Democracy is not allowed because God doesn't judge according to the democratic method. It is not a statement used to reject people judging you, it is for replacing or revising the standard you are judged by. Basically it means "*Only judge me the way God would, not how you or others want. Only judge me as God wants you to judge me.*" Yet sadly the popular catchphrase is typically used when a wrongdoer doesn't want to be corrected, out of arrogance. Most who use it ironically use it to reject the judgment of God because they don't like condemnation for being sinful. Rather than say "*Only God can Judge me*" one should say, "*You can only judge me according to the law of God.*"

I used to ignorantly imagine revolutions could be beneficial, although now I know why it is impossible for a revolution to result in improvement. The word "revolution" itself reveals it is nothing but destructive. For example if you put a sticker on a wheel and then the wheel goes through one revolution, the sticker will end up at the same spot it was at before the revolution began except both the sticker and wheel will be worn and in a worse condition. If you had an old tire on a car that was in a bad state, a revolution would not improve the wheel; it would only damage it further making it less useful and more unstable. If you want to get a better wheel, you get a different wheel entirely, putting the wheel through revolutions only continues the problem by wearing out the rubber. Political revolutions are the same as wheel revolutions, some bad politicians are rubbed out just as the tire of a car wheel is rubbed off in the rotation, but the bad politicians were only a part of the wheel. Removing them doesn't fix the wheel, the wheel must be changed. This is why if you look at the recent revolutions that have taken place, those countries are worse off today than they were before the revolutions. Likewise the vast overwhelming majority of revolutionary groups fail because they are incapable of predicting/preventing/combatting the inter-revolutionary warfare amongst rival revolutionary groups since they start with the delusion that a revolution is binary with only two parties, oblivious to the fact that every revolution has had many many parties jockeying for total victory over all the rest. As a result typically due to their inability to defeat both the ruling class and the other revolutionary parties the revolutionary populace ends up with the incumbent suppressing all the revolutionaries together or one at a time contrary to their hopes/dreams/achievements. Every single revolution, even the peaceful type, has been a multi-faceted civil war. Truly there is no such thing as singular binary revolutions between 2 parties, there are always a plethora of people/ideas/faiths/groups always trying to achieve dominance commonly within the same groups making it extremely confusing and difficult for any particular sect to achieve it's goals in full. Hence most revolutions just lead to greater disunity, especially if they aren't done prophetically. Seeing as the wheel symbolizes government, even if instead of a revolution a different wheel were tried in the form of a different political system, a different wheel won't necessarily solve the problem. A rubber wheel will wear out sooner or later and cause problems regardless of what brand it is, or what mixture of rubber it is. Therefore the vehicle of humanity needs perfect tires that will last forever. No human can make such a tire, humans didn't make the species or environment either. Since every other part that drives humanity forward has been made by the Creator, the only tires that will propel the human species are those made by the Creator. The wheels being a symbol of political and government systems means that only a divinely ordained political or government system will work. Every man-made tire will expire and wreck the car if it's not continuously replaced. God has made a form of government for mankind and that's the only solution. No revolution will bring any long-term benefit to mankind. Humans are prone to error, therefore a man-made government system will be prone to error. If you want a good government you have to go to the Creator of goodness. The only good government is one where the laws of God are the laws the people are governed by. Any other government is invalid and will cause nothing but misery for those living under it. It is the Jews who believe *"The law of the land is the law."* which they preach with their phrase *"Dina demal khuta dian"* Muslims do not believe that whatever laws the land is ruled by are legitimate laws just because they are used. The existence of a legal code does not amount to legal legitimacy. Although just because a government is invalid doesn't mean a Muslim can disobey its laws. When a Muslim is in a certain country they are bound to uphold their promise to abide by the laws of that country which don't conflict with Islam. For instance most traffic laws don't conflict with Islam so those types of laws can and should be followed. Yet just because a Muslim follows the laws that don't conflict with Islam doesn't mean they recognize the government, its legislation or judiciary to be valid for even a milisecond. Following the law doesn't mean respecting the lawmakers, or acknowledging them as legitimate authority figures. Just as following the laws of God doesn't mean a person loves God or believes in God. On the other hand someone cannot respect the lawmakers if they don't obey the law. Likewise a person cannot love God if they don't obey the divine laws. To sin is to prove you don't really love God while you are sinning, to obey and believe in God is to prove your love via living it. Love for God shows itself through your actions as does lack of love for God. People didn't make the earth or any of the elements in it for themselves. The world is basically rented to mankind for a short amount of time. Part of the rental agreement contains certain clauses for the rules concerning governing of the world. God has appointed humans to be custodians of the earth. Custodians have rules to follow in order to do their job. If the custodians aren't following the rules of their employer then they won't be doing their job correctly and the object they are custodian over will suffer, making their job harder and joyless, leading to eventual termination by the employer for not doing the job they were appointed to do. The earth is the property of God. In order for mankind to act as custodian over God's property they have to follow the rules God has made for the earth. If the owner of a building says no fires are allowed on the property and they hire a custodian to take care of the building, the custodian has no right to change the rules and say fires are allowed on the property. Even though the custodian has authority to do their job, that authority is limited and conditional to them following the rules of the property owner. This means any government who exercises authority and rules over God's land must rule by the laws God has legislated, as should we in ruling ourself. If a government were to prohibit something God has commanded, or to legalize something God has forbidden then that government is unacceptable, invalid and blameworthy. This is why participating in the legal systems of secular or democratic governments is so sinful and can potentially make one a disbeliever if they think it isn't.

Man-made laws are like grass, too many to count and they get chopped up by people in milliseconds. If people don't like the grass then they just cover it up to ignore it or take it out and plant different grass instead, then when the political seasons change all the laws die and the cold grip of a police state covers the land like the snow, until the seasons change again and new grass grows repeating the cycle of oppressive unjust instablity. With many thinking the grass will always be greener if they just added another blade or removed another blade thinking that if they just have a good system to select a good gardener then winter will never come and they won't be oppressed. Yet God is the gardener we should have and the one who controls the weather and political seasons causing snow as well as oppressive governments so people learn that choosing to live by man-made laws results in fruitless and dangerous winters. God has perfected his garden for us with the final prophet to add the final flowers to the landscape of legislation for humanity. Where if we choose to tend the worldly garden God has given us according to God's instructions, then when we leave this temporary garden we will live forever in heavenly gardens that we don't have to tend. Otherwise we will be burning forever for having slashed and burned in order to customize the worldly garden God entrusted to us and specifically told us how to maintain. It's simple, God gave us life and laws, if we don't follow the laws that God gave us to live our lives by we won't have a good life or afterlife. Many laws made by governments today are illegal in the sight of God. Such a simple statement of pure noble truth would be considered a "*threat to national security*" by many criminal governments across the world. To such a government "security" means the taxation status quo. "*National Security*" is typically defined as government authority, it has nothing to do with protecting the economic interests of a country, the personal safety of its citizens, or the environment; unless threats to those things would threaten the taxation system and government authority. The government is not your "big brother" or your "Uncle Sam". Even if they were family, family only cares about you to a limited extent. Most governments in the world don't care about your security in the afterlife. Most governments don't care whether you spend eternity in hell. The man-made laws are not designed to protect you from hell. If the laws of your country are not the laws of God then you can be a law-abiding citizen in the sight of your government, yet a criminal in the sight of God. This is why it is important to have religious government. Throughout history secular governments created environments of sin and immorality. Today we have countries where a "model citizen" can be a disbelieving sinner who possesses all the attributes of a person who will spend eternity in hell, but the secular government portrays them as a good person or role model. If you look at secular countries like America, sin is legalized. In America a person will get in more trouble for a traffic violation than they will for breaking the laws ordained by the Creator of the universe! The priorities of American politicians are wrong. The goal of a government should be to protect its citizens from disbelief and sin. Of course a government can't force belief upon a person and that is against the religion of Islam, but a government can and should prevent sin from becoming rampant in its domain. Instead most secular governments tell their subjects they have "freedom", essentially giving them a license to sin. That is what "freedom" is, it's a license to sin. Sin is sin, God has given governments temporary authority over others so they can protect people from sin, not so they could legalize it. Unfortunately secular governments do the opposite of what governments are supposed to do and they profit from sin. If it weren't for the revenue from taxes on pornography, prostitution, alcohol, drugs, gambling and all other vices and evils of society, secular governments would be broke. In every secular country you will find the same, sin has become industrialized and ties into the interests of the secular governments. Such governments actively promote a sinful culture because if people were moral it would mean lower tax revenue and smaller government budgets. For secular governments it is actually in their interest for you to sin. A secular government essentially wants you to disobey God and burn in hell. Satan has deployed secularism as a tool to mislead mankind from the true religion. As much as Satan invests in false religions, because they are religions it still makes people think religion and worship are important, even though they are doing it all wrong. For Satan humans even caring about religion is risky, because one who cares about religion can still be guided to the true religion if they grow up upon a false religion. The satanic idea of secularism was promoted under the guise of interfaith coexistence and peace, but the real reason and effects of this have been to dilute religion and eliminate morality from humanity altogether. Of course Satan will fail to eliminate the true religion, but by diluting religions Satan hopes to cause deviance, negligence and laziness among the believers. So even if a person finds the true religion, because the secular world sees religion as unimportant and extreme, they may not fully practice the true religion. That is Satan's goal, to stop people from fully practicing the true religion, he knows he will never stop people from believing in it, but technically if you believe in the true religion you would practice it fully. Unfortunately this secular trend has led many to end up believing in one religion but in reality not practicing any religion. This is where the other type of extremism shows its face. Satan wants disbelief and extremism. Just as Satan makes more than 1 false religion, Satan makes more than 1 extremism to offer more roads to hell to mislead more people.

It's not extreme to admit a theological and physical war is going on, that's called honesty and shows a solution is desired. Getting labeled extreme can make one numb to the idea until eventually the person becomes extremely deviant one way or the other, if they don't remain firm and steadfast upon the truth. One can only practice the true religion and avoid extremes if they stop caring about what people say and think about them, instead focusing solely on pleasing their Creator. The religion of God is not extreme, but to disbelievers and extremists it will be considered extreme. Regardless if we consider hellfire and heaven, these are two extremes. One is extremely bad and one is extremely good. It is only natural that such extreme destinations would be reached through what seem to be extreme means. Either one is extremely good and goes to paradise or extremely bad and goes to hell.

Either your belief is perfectly correct and complete, or totally false and wrong. God doesn't have a permanent place for the average person where they experience both pain and pleasure forever. It's one or the other, either eternal torture or eternal pleasure. The test of life has extremely high stakes, therefore in a sense the religion of God is extreme, it is extremely good and important. Just as the opinions of people should not be valued over the opinion of God, the opinions of illegitimate governments who don't rule by the law of God should also be devoid of influence over us. Rather than care if something is politically correct, we should be concerned if something is religiously correct. Out of all the prophets I know of I don't know of any whom the disbelievers considered to be "politically correct". Pharaoh threatened the magicians who repented, reformed and followed Moses pbuh with a torturous death because they believed. Yet the believers were steadfast in doing what was right, worshipping God alone in the correct way. Thus Pharaoh said he must kill them to protect the citizens, justifying his actions by saying he was terrified of their assault on the beliefs, values and way of life which the Egyptian people held dear for centuries. But pause. Most people will tell the story of Moses pbuh and Pharaoh in the course of a few minutes or hours, but keep in mind this interaction took place over the course of many years. Moses pbuh didn't enter Egypt, show his signs, get rejected and then flee across the Sea all in one day, his mission took years to finish. So regarding religious revival and establishment one must be extremely patient while traveling that prophetic path. If anything or anyone is preventing us from taking that path, we can't turn around or stop traveling the road to paradise as a result, because since time keeps moving it means we are always moving on the road to paradise or the roads to hell. Most social pressure will either cause us to leave the road to paradise, shift gears on the road to paradise so we stay in the same place without moving while spinning our wheels wasting energy, or cause us to go in reverse on the road to paradise making us farther from our goal as time passes. But in reality regardless of whether we let the negative social pressure affect us or not, there will be pressure. Therefore we should make sure that the pressure is positive and that the environment we are in motivates us and promotes us going to the finish line on the road to paradise. The solution for sinful environments is a government based on the religion of God. I don't think such a state will come about through revolutions or force. If it ever did it wouldn't last or be secure. The way to have a government structured by the laws of God is if people accept the authority of God and want to practice the religion of God, then demand a government that establishes the religion of God which protects them from sin. This requires human interaction and communication and lots of patience. Most people are ignorant and simply don't know what the true religion is, and not all who do know it practice it. If people practiced the true religion and shared it with others, it would flourish. This is what the prophets pbut did. Primarily we have to start with ourselves, how can you possibly be a happy citizen of a country governed by the laws of God if you personally disobey the laws of God publicly or privately? How can you live in a country where the laws of God are the laws of the land if the laws of God aren't obeyed within your own household? Fundamental steps are required. I must practice the true religion before I can share it with others. Then others must practice it before they can share it. Then many must practice it before it can be established throughout the land. You don't have to be sinless before you share Islam with others, else none would ever share it, but it is important to practice what one preaches and have knowledge about what one teaches. If you don't know, then say you don't know. If you don't practice a particular aspect then when telling others to do so keep in mind your ears are closer to your mouth than their ears are, so speak your words to yourself while directing them towards others. If many people practiced the true religion, then it would peacefully become the model for a government system because even disbelievers would see the justice of it and want to live under the laws of God. This is how Muhammad pbuh established the Islamic State in Madinah. The prophet Muhammad pbuh practiced Islam in Mecca and told some travelers from Madinah about it. Those travelers became Muslim and practiced Islam when they returned to Madinah. Eventually people in Madinah voluntarily became Muslims and practiced Islam. Later Muhammad pbuh was requested to come live in Madinah and be its leader by both Muslims and non-Muslims. This is the way Muhammad pbuh peacefully established an Islamic State governed by Shariah, simply by practicing Islam and sharing it with others. The true prophetic religion of Islam can never be forced upon people it must be voluntarily accepted.

Law in itself is an exclusively religious construct. That doesn't mean that all laws come from God, but all law comes into existence from religion or religions. Therefore after explaining that fundamental truth I explain that as such if there is a law better than Islamic Shariah then it can only come from a religion that is better than Islam. While if there were a religion better than Islam that gives a law better than Shariah, it would mean Islam is not the best religion and as such cannot be the true prophetic religion of God. However when we then **scholastically** compare Islamic Shariah to any other government system or legal code, every single time the people have agreed that their system has flaws in which Islamic Shariah is better and superior. Furthermore anything good about any unislamic legal code was likely copied from the Islamic Shariah and it's a proven fact, not just a claim. Even colonial America incorporated Islamic Shariah into the American Law, but they didn't want to publicly say they copied it. Yet in the Supreme Court they have a engraving allegedly depicting Muhammad pbuh because of his positive influence on American law. Muslims and non-Muslims in America both want this engraving destroyed, for different reasons, but it doesn't get destroyed because the Court insists they want to acknowledge the beneficial influence of

Muhammad pbuh on American law or rather the fact that they copied parts of Shariah law but don't say so. Those who oppose Shariah law don't even know what it is except for the famous penalties for adultery or theft. Although why would someone who doesn't steal or commit adultery have a problem with Shariah's laws regarding the treatment of thieves or adulterers? Really if they aren't thieves or adulterers then even if they hate the notion of adulterers or thieves being sternly punished under Shariah it will never happen to them so they don't have to worry about it. As these anti-shariah types always say to Muslims, "*If you got nothing to hide and aren't a terrorist then why worry about surveillance?*" So one can pose this same type of question to opponents of Shariah for almost every aspect of it they oppose. For example if they aren't sodomites then it shouldn't matter to them that Shariah punishes sodomy and if they aren't sinful people then Shariah will never harm them in any way. The problem is that Shariah does legally forbid certain popular vices, like gambling, cheating, lying, slandering, smoking, buying/selling intoxicants. Within Shariah violent corporal punishments only amount to maybe 2-5% of Shariah law and they are rarely applied, just as the death penalty is rarely applied in secular states which have the death penalty for certain crimes today. Yet how many who disagree with the death penalty also demand the country's entire legal code be abolished because of that one tiny legal aspect of criminal law which they might dislike? Nobody, they acknowledge that's just one tiny thread of a whole tapestry. So even if there was something which a non-Muslim doesn't like about Shariah, first of all it most likely will never effect them and secondly no entire system can be rejected just because of 1 aspect of that system. If an entire legal code is to be rejected then there must be a fundamental reason to reject it all, but never can a tiny aspect of something be a valid reason to condemn the entirety of it. Just as 1 bad apple doesn't ruin the bunch, 1 bad law doesn't invalidate a legal system. Now I'm not saying Shariah has any bad laws, I don't believe it does but what I am saying is that you can't delegitimize any system based on bits and pieces of it. The apple analogy is appropriate. The reason the unislamic legal systems are condemned is not necessarily because a few apples(laws) are toxic or a few bad branches of government exist, or due to a few bad leaves(politicians), but because the apples were grown from the tree Allah has forbidden us to utilize and the foundational seeds(doctrines) are satanic in their origin. So when the seed from which a government is planted is sinful then the government that grows upon those principles will be a sinful tree resulting in poisonous consequences with the roots ruining the earth and the growth of the tree blocking out the light of Allah spreading devilish darkness where light once was. It is a Christian concept that "you will know them by the fruits they produce", Islam decrees that the fruits can reveal much about the tree but fundamentally you study the seeds which planted the tree and ignore the tree basing your decision on whether to keep the tree or not based on the seed it grew from not the fruits it produces or it's appearance or the strength of it's roots or popularity throughout the land. Sadly though most non-Muslims judge governments solely by their fruits and only the famous fruits rather than all the fruits and they think new leaves will fix the problems the various branches of government are responsible for. Democracy basically teaches that leaves can cure or corrupt an entire tree. One key problem which non-Muslims have with Shariah is that they've never tasted any of its fruits directly from the tree and only hear of the taste of the notorious fruits which to them seem bitter because their tastebuds are attuned to thinking injustice tastes sweet. Most possess zero experiential knowledge regarding the matter, and most have zero knowledge of any type regarding Shariah. Thus they are biased and prejudiced. Yet Shariah produces many fruits and not everyone will taste them all since it is impossible to do since certain laws only apply to certain people in certain situations. Thus the problem with the kuffar is they desire the fruits of the trees that grew from seeds planted by Satan and as such fear the taste of trees from the seeds planted by God and his prophets. In reality nobody ever tastes all the fruits of a legal system so their judgements are based on theories and prejudices, which is fine if the decisions were made based on the seeds. Yet unfortunately their decisions are based on the fruits of which they haven't tasted from both trees so they always will make the wrong decision until they taste Shariah or learn more about it. Those who do learn more than 5 things about Shariah law say it's great. They find it fascinating how just and modernly applicable it is for being around for over 1400 years. Some people even go so far as to say that they want to live under Islamic Shariah and they aren't even Muslims. The well-informed non-Muslims actually support Shariah law, but typically since after becoming informed they become Muslim then their opinion, desire and reasoning is discounted by non-Muslims. One time a foreign business partner wrote me in regards to banking that, "*I am a Christian at heart but would never deal with a institution that does not practise Shariah law.*" Thus as a non-Muslim who can choose other than Shariah, he still freely chooses Shariah law simply because to him, despite his religious beliefs, Shariah compliant institutions are better than all the rest. So this is where any Muslims who assimilate within unislamic environments are actually degrading Islam. There is nothing about Islam that Muslims can be ashamed of, rather it's non-Muslims and unislamic Muslims who feel shame when they genuinely compare their beliefs and ways with Islam.

You don't vote for a "lesser evil" and not become responsible for that evil. If you vote then that makes you partially responsible for everything that person does or would've done. There is no distinction between a vote cast by one who supports 100% of a politician's plans and a vote cast by one who supports 0% but just doesn't want someone else to win. The intentions behind the votes don't matter, all votes are equal as per the dogma. Whereas the Quran commands Muslims to not help/support one another in evil and wrongdoing. Islam doesn't teach Muslims to support the lesser evil, it sternly commands us DO NOT SUPPORT EVIL! That means Muslims don't vote for disbelievers or in democratic elections in non-Muslim lands because it's an evil system and by voting one is contributing to wrongdoing and evil. Voting for anybody in a democracy is active support of the democratic system and allegiance to those politicians and Islam forbids such support and allegiance. It's simple if you don't believe in democracy then you don't vote in the elections. To vote means that you believe in the system and are trying to use it. You cannot vote for a leader you hate, it's impossible to do. When people vote for a "lesser evil" they are simply choosing which rope to hang themselves with. They are voting for their oppressor and as such become directly responsible for their own oppression because of voting. Not voting frees you from responsibility, voting to prevent another oppressor from "winning" still makes one responsible for oppression and the desire for oppression. Meaning even if the person one votes for doesn't win and the "greater evil" wins, the voter would still be responsible and guilty for all the evil stuff the other one would've done had they been elected. Thus by voting the voter loses spiritually in the afterlife even if the one they voted for "loses", unless they repent from the sin of voting.

Why is it that you are only allowed to vote for the politicians of a nation and not the policies it has or abandons? The reason democracies postulate voting for leaders is because if the people are left to govern themselves it's known they would make the wrong decisions. However with that being the case then automatically that means the voters will also make the wrong decision when voting for their leaders. If the reason people vote is due to the tendency of the masses to make the wrong choice then it's also wrong to let them vote for a leader because they will make the wrong choice in that regard too. Thus democracy is a contradictory system where for voting to be right it has to simultaneously be wrong to vote. If the people can't be trusted to vote for the right decision on every policy then they can't be trusted to vote for the right politician in an election. Democracy refutes itself. Yet not only are voters not allowed to pick policies to vote for, nor the candidates but the government itself tells the people what the issues the candidates are to differ over are. People living under democracies or pseudo-democracies can't even get an honest debate between candidates because most government policies aren't up for discussion, like the issue of military alliances or taxation. Furthermore because being a leader is such a large responsibility which most people will fail to do without sinning or committing injustice, then it follows that good religious people don't want the risk of leadership due to the dangers they'll face in the afterlife for being a bad leader. Due to this any person who desires leadership is disqualified from it because the only ones who desire to take the spiritual risk of the responsibility leadership entails must be either crazy or corrupt and both possibilities indicate a bad leader. Therefore in Islam anyone who wants to become the leader is automatically rejected as a possible candidate to be the leader, since any who want the job are guaranteed to do a bad job because they don't fear doing a bad job, if they did they wouldn't want the job. Any person campaigning to be elected as a leader is automatically not qualified to be the leader and will certainly do a bad job of it. So democratic elections are schematically designed to give a nation the worst most power-hungry possible candidates. The worst way to get a leader is to ask "Who wants to be the leader?" and then select one of those. Hence democracy always results in bad evil leaders. In Islam the people of knowledge and influence force an individual to be the leader of their nation because they are the best person and the people won't let them not be the leader. While in democracy people are forced to pick a leader out of those who are eager for the position, the good ones who don't want leadership never become the leaders. It's truly amazing every election because you have politicians who none of the people would want to marry, nor raise their kids, nor have as a business partner yet they vote for them to govern them. Why? Because those politicians said they wanted the job AND the government agreed to let them apply. Yet years earlier none of the voters would have picked those politicians for the job. The voters wouldn't even have known their names if they hadn't started a campaign. It is the politician who preaches they are the best for the job first, then the government agrees to let them participate in the election as a candidate and then people agree they should/could be the leader, mainly due to the poor quality of every other applicant which the government agreed could participate as a candidate. The voters never truly choose to vote for X, instead X chooses them to vote for X and the government's candidates A-Z just gave the voters a less persuasive salespitch. What the masses of people should do is not vote and send a message to these politicians explaining: "*None of you are qualified to be the type of good leader we truly need and deserve. None of you get the job. We will search for someone else because all of you politician's suck. None of us are voting so all of you lose and do not get elected because the election is cancelled, due to inferior candidates who do not fit minimum criteria to be a good leader. We'd rather keep the position vacant than fill it with anyone of you con-artist tyrants. Perhaps the government will be closed until we find quality leaders. If we can't find any good citizens then maybe we will appoint a foreigner if our country is that corrupt as it appears thus far. As sad as it is, we might actually need to import a good leader for us because honestly our country might not have any good leaders among us and we want a good leader rather than a native leader. We want the best leader in the world. We don't want the best of us. To get the best you have to be the best and we might not be the best, and if not then we are going to get the best even if it's a foreigner. Sometimes the best leader for your country isn't born in your country, doesn't live there and doesn't currently have citizenship. The best country gets the best leader regardless of their location. Being the leader of our great country is too important to vote on. We cannot risk our nation by putting leadership to a popular vote.*" In Islam the leader is forced by the people to lead against his will because of the will of the knowledgeable people, while under democracy the masses of stupid people are forced to pick a leader they don't want to lead according to the leader's will. Under Islam the people of knowledge and influence choose their leader in a type of meritocracy, under democracy the leaders make the stupid masses of people theoretically choose them. Linguistically it may sound similar, but under Islam God made the law already and clarifies the criteria of selecting which few good people get to pick the leader who is just supposed to do as God says leaders are supposed to do, namely make sure nobody violates the laws of God and protect the nation from its enemies. Under democracy the leaders make the law and do what people allegedly want contrary to what God says they should do and every idiot gets a say in who gets to do such a bad job of governing. Under Islamic Shariah nobody wants to be the leader because the leader is a servant and slave of God and the people, but under unislamic systems the people are the slaves of the leader who usurps the authority of God. The reason democracy is from the devil is because it is literally the people picking their own leader who make their own laws, in opposition to the leaders God desires them to have and the legal code God has ordained. Since we are always repeating that God is the one to judge and the opinion of people doesn't matter why then do we judge who our leaders are and allow the opinion of people to determine both our leaders and our laws? For God to be the only judge means that people have no right to pick their own leader via popular opinion or elections. Why doesn't God allow democracy? Because we are stupid sinners. How can people who routinely elect to sin possibly ever elect a decent leader? Before the masses can be qualified to pick a good leader they have to be able to live a good lifestyle. If they choose to be evil sinners then they will always choose evil leaders. Which since the masses are always evil sinners then whenever the masses get to pick their leader they will select one that is evil because for the masses choosing evil is habitual. Hence it has always been the case for every democratic election that people have said "*vote for the lesser of 2 evils*" and what does it get them? It results in evil. Maybe if people decided not to vote for a "lesser evil" we might actually get a result that is not evil. It's worth a try, because if everybody doesn't vote then nobody wins the election and the system peacefully ceases to exist as a legitimate political ritual to initiate a ceremonial changing of government mascots. The sad thing is that nobody in democratic countries who hears the slogan "*vote for the lesser of 2 evils*" seems to make the correct decision. When you are living in a country where everyone agrees that the next leader will be evil no matter who it is and they only disagree on which potential leader is less evil, then the correct decision for you is to get out of that country which you know is going to have an evil leader. Do I have to say it? Why don't people just add evil + evil = It's time to leave. Vote with your feet. Don't wait for the results when you already know the end result is evil. You wouldn't pick your poison would you? That's satanic. So then why do people pick their politicians? What happened to people that they decided instead of fighting the forces of evil, they choose to vote for the lesser evil? The problem is they got patriotic and are too attached to a certain section of dirt which they live on. They fell in love with dirt and decided they love that dirt patch so much they are sticking to it for as long as they live because their evil leaders tricked them into thinking every other country is ruled by even greater evil, or they are afraid of losing money or the companionship of other humans who live on the same pile of dirt as they do. Thus they decide to live under evil together rather than fight the evil or move elsewhere. They'd rather be slaves working the soil than fight to improve their lives on the soil, if it means risking death and burial under the soil. They'd rather be trampled and disgraced above the soil than buried with honor under it. When you have such stupid satanic materialism, it's no wonder they have evil satanic leaders. Evil people don't rule good people. God has never told mankind to vote for evil and God does not want people to vote for evil. Just ask a pro-voting for evil person if

God told them to vote for evil or if it was Satan? Imagine Satan's #1 devil and his #2 devil were pitted against each other in an election. Would you vote for one of Satan's devils? Would you vote for Satan's #2 devil to be your leader? Do you think a prophet would? Actually we know the answer to this. In Mecca the Muslims were horribly persecuted and when the leader Abu Talib died, Muhammad pbuh being a member of the Quraysh tribe had the right to vote for who would be the next leader of Mecca. All the electable candidates were disbelievers and hostile to Islam. Know that whenever Muhammad pbuh was faced with 2 options he always chose the easier option as long as it didn't involve sin. As a member of the tribe Muhammad pbuh could've been elected leader of the city. So did Muhammad pbuh vote for himself? No, because he didn't believe in democracy and voting is sinful. So an enemy of Islam was elected to be leader of Mecca and the Muslims were persecuted even worse than before, yet still Muhammad pbuh never voted nor did he tell Muslims to vote for him or a "lesser evil" despite knowing persecution would increase in different levels based on who got elected. He had a chance to vote for the "lesser evil" or himself in an election that impacted all Muslims and he choose not to. So from this one can know the correct prophetic example for Muslims to follow during elections in a non-Muslim country is to not vote, but practice Islam trying to implement it there while also looking for alternative places to preach Islam where the people are more likely to embrace or implement Islam more fully. Every alleged democracy is a sinking ship, economically, politically, morally and spiritually, and all democracies if there ever were any are sinking ships of a false religion anyways. Yet people ask "*Who do you want to win the election?*" so I reply, "*When you are in a sinking ship full of holes that cannot be repaired then who cares who wins the election to be the next Captain? The boat is sinking! It's not time to choose a new leader, if you want to solve the problem you gotta get a whole new boat. If you take part in the vote for a new leader then you are part of the problem.*" Truthfully

Muslims are not supposed to be in the non-Muslim lands to influence the system, we are suppose to share the guidance of Islam and implement the Islamic system as best as we can while rejecting the unislamic beliefs and systems. Muslims can't be voting year after year and then say, "*Ok now that we are a majority, we vote that there are no more elections, time for Shariah*". That's dishonest hypocrisy and not how Islam works, Shariah doesn't come via surprise. Muslims live to campaign for Allah, not for kafirs. You cannot use any system to abolish itself. The Muslims in Muslim countries can't even get Shariah by voting and their nations' constitutions say Islam is the official state religion, so for Muslims to think they will vote Shariah into place in kafir countries where the constitutions and state religions promote freedom and secularism is completely delusional. They will more likely be eliminated via genocide than achieve victory via democracy. Good deeds result in good, evil deeds result in evil. If voting results in evil then such a vote would be evil. Regardless of whether the results are good or evil, the results themselves do not determine good deeds. The results do identify evil deeds but not good deeds. Bad deeds can have good results but good deeds never result in evil. There are black, white and gray deeds, the gray deeds are not good deeds so don't do them. Voting is something that makes Satan happy, and since people die every second, you don't want to be one who dies voting or intends to vote; especially voting for evil. Likewise voting results in more than 1 type of sin because on the way to the polls and at the polling place one is likely going to see and hear sinful things due to people being dressed improperly or speaking sinful speech. So one's eyes, ears and mouth can gets sins due to the voting process. Thus even if voting wasn't sinful it becomes sinful due to the sins that are involved in the process. Over a lifetime the amount of total time spent by voters on elections(and I'm including all the pre-election drama, thinking, debating, research etc) adds up to days/weeks worth of life. People literally spend days/weeks/months of their life voting for evil. That's not what God wants people to do with their time, hence voting is also sinful because it's a terrible waste of your life. Then when you multiply that time spent per each voter this is trillions of hours wasted by voters which they could've used to do something useful and good. Good people are too busy doing good deeds to vote. Seriously even if voting weren't sinful, I don't have time to vote anyways. Change doesn't happen via voting, that's not the way Allah changes things. Allah tells Muslims he never changes the condition of people until they change their inner selves. Voting is the problem, not a solution or a way to prevent problems. If people did something God likes instead of focusing on voting then the world would be fixed. Following the prophets is the solution for us, not voting for politicians. The politicians are false prophets. The one who believes in God doesn't cast a vote because it's a sin of the first degree. Truly the politicians are prophets whom people think are the means of their salvation, voting is a religious ritual where you end up picking a devil dressed in human clothing thinking that will prevent another devil from ruling. But after the votes are counted the end result is people voted for a devil to govern them, and God does not reward voting. Isn't it extreme to say that elected politicians are devils? That depends. They'd be devils if they believe that human changes to laws will fix things. Are there any elected politicians who don't believe that? I don't think so, but maybe; on another planet. Any leader who accepts being appointed by the result of a popular election is unfit to lead. The reason elections always involve voting for a "lesser evil" is because voting itself is evil and only allows evil options. At the end of this dispute of voting, it's either forbidden or not. If it is forbidden what are the potential consequences a voter faces in the afterlife? If it's not then what rewards would they get for voting, in the afterlife? Now if someone doesn't vote will God punish them? After answering these three questions it becomes clear that the risk of voting and it being sinful far outweighs any potential benefit voting could bring. So the risk/reward ratio says don't vote, especially since it's not obligatory to vote and it's not a sin to abstain. The fact that people ask about whether they should vote is proof enough that it is sinful and politically useless, because their heart is telling them it is and at the very least it's a doubtful matter. Whereas Muhammad pbuh taught that the lawful is clear and the sinful is clear while in between that there are doubtful matters, of which the successful one in the afterlife avoids the doubtful matters and/or inquires about the doubtful by asking the knowledgeable to explain so it is no longer doubtful. Since at the minimum it's doubtful as to whether voting is permissible or sinful or disbelief and it's known 100% that it's not sinful to not vote, then it becomes clear that not voting is lawful while voting is sinful or doubtful. Hence the successful person who goes to paradise according to Muhammad pbuh does not vote in democratic elections. You have literally nothing to lose by not voting and so so much to lose by voting, just don't do it. Don't risk a place in paradise by casting a vote which can put you in eternal hell. Not even 1 prophet ever voted in a democratic election, especially for a disbeliever, so just do what the prophets did and don't vote. The footsteps of the prophets do not lead to voting stations. Dua is more effective and that's something God actually loves and rewards us for. From day 1 Muslims must be open about our intentions, just as Muhammad pbuh was and all the prophets were. Jesus pbuh could have ran for political office and become a Senator in Rome and maybe even Emperor, but he didn't. While Moses pbuh could have chosen to work for the Egyptian government and become the next Pharaoh, which was entirely realistic and pragmatic since he was the adopted son of the Pharaoh. Moses pbuh had a legitimate chance at legally ruling all of Egypt through peaceful succession if he just kept quiet and worked the system for a few years; but he didn't. While another example of Jesus pbuh is how he dealt with the Jewish political/religious structure. For example with democratic "Islamic Societies" that are in control of some masjids, are those exceptions which Muslims can participate in and "work the system, changing it from the inside" if it's an unislamic or democratic system but run by Muslims? Well Jesus pbuh lived in such a time where the religious temples and rabbis in the holy land were based on unislamic systems in religious guises with religious names for them, but Jesus pbuh never ever joined the hypocritical Jewish political systems; rather he openly opposed them. The Jews used to vote for the Rabbis who would manage the Temple but Jesus pbuh didn't participate nor vote. Jesus pbuh didn't preach Jewish unity against the Romans, he preached that you side with the truth against all falsehood regardless of the odds stacked against you, even if it makes the enemies of your enemies ally with each other against you. With his miracles and wisdom Jesus pbuh could have easily climbed the Jewish political and clerical ladder and became the head Rabbi of the Temple of Jerusalem in a few years time and then consolidated power and liberated the holy land from Roman occupation, but doing so would mean compromising the truth and accepting unislamic political systems and working with hypocrites so he didn't. Muslims don't "work unislamic political systems" thereby imitating the disbelievers, we come with the truth and divine system to abolish the falsehood of all man-made systems. Muslims come to abolish not to polish. If the Western people would just talk with us and after learning Islam and Shariah they decide collectively they don't want to be Muslims or implement Shariah, then the Muslims will leave them and go to the Muslim countries. The problem is the disbelievers don't want to actually learn about Islam or Shariah and many Muslims in the West don't want to move, thus this conversation doesn't happen on a national scale as it should. Peacefully we should be able to come to a reasonable conclusion. Proper Muslims will not assimilate, the Islamic system is superior according to our beliefs and critical analysis so we are trying to upgrade the world with Islam. An easy pitch for Muslims to prove that Democracy is evil is to simply say: *"Why is it that whenever there is a democratic election people always say to "vote for the lesser of two evils"? If Democracy were truly good then shouldn't people be asking every single election how people will vote between "the best of many goods"? Wouldn't the best form of government mean the spot of leadership always goes to the "best of the best people"? If the system continuously makes your leader be the "lesser evil of evil people" then that is a very evil system of government that must be replaced as soon as possible. Muslims believe Shariah is God's solution to democracy and all evil forms of government. We think everyone is unique and not equal and that the best people should have more authority in making decisions. In particular those who believe in God correctly and follow the religion taught by all of God's prophets. We don't think people who are immoral and don't believe in God should have an equal say in government as someone who is moral and correctly believes in and obeys God. So no Islam does not promote equality or democracy, but rejects those political notions because we believe the best people should be in charge and get selected by the best people according to God's criteria of good and bad, and that wealth, race, nationality, or popularity have nothing to do with qualifications for leadership. The majority of people are not qualified to choose the best candidate to lead a country or the best decision that God would want, so we don't believe in majority vote decisions when it comes to political leaders or political decisions. Muslims believe that a government based upon a majority of votes by the majority of people will make terrible decisions and get terrible leaders the majority of the time. "* Now religiously the West doesn't think they need an upgrade and thinks the Muslims are the ones needing an upgraded ideology, values and legal system. However if the West lets us preach to them then we'll preach, if they don't allow us to preach in their lands then we will leave. The core problem at the moment is the non-Muslims don't really want Shariah anywhere at all. So they don't want Muslims in the West to preach Islam, nor do they want us to leave and establish Shariah in our own territories, they just want us to change our beliefs. That's okay, but sooner or later something and some people will have to change, the modern situation cannot go on as it is forever. For instance when Moses pbuh came to Pharaoh in Egypt, immediately he asked him to change his religion and implement Allah's legal system, if Pharaoh choose not to then he was told he should let the believers leave. Moses pbuh was clear from day 1, yet in the end Pharaoh neither believed nor let the believers leave. The situation today is much the same except not all the Muslims in the West know Islam and are sending mixed messages and some don't even practice Islam. The Muslims today aren't as they were when with Moses pbuh, but then again the Pharaohs aren't the same either. The Muslims didn't want to rule pagan Egypt, yet that's what Pharaoh feared and told people. The enemies of Islam play the same game today, trying to make people afraid of some subversive Muslim takeover. Any such alleged plots themselves are anti-Islamic. Proper Stable Islamic Shariah doesn't happen via secrecy or surprise.

Religion is more than just beliefs, it also covers economics, politics, morals, laws, government etc. Now everybody in the world knows there are problems with those things in the world today and are dissatisfied searching for solutions that don't work or make things worse. We simply cannot solve religious problems without also solving political/economic/social problems and we cannot solve the political/economic/social problems without solving the religious problems. The world problems are a package deal and the solution is likewise a package deal. Intending to only solve some of the world problems is not the solution. The only solution that will work is to solve all the problems as the prophets pbut taught us to do. While to do that we definitely need help and guidance from the Creator of the Universe. Hence religion is the only solution and only the true religion will fix the world 100%. Yet when preaching the true religion one cannot ignore the world problems and give the impression that beliefs about God are the only issue and political, economic, social problems aren't something you are trying to fix with your religion. If one is to say someone is wrong about their beliefs concerning God then it's easy to tell them they are wrong about everything else too. In fact suggesting someone is wrong about God should be the most offensive thing to people, because that's the easiest thing to understand out of everything in the world. If you don't know God then you don't know nothing. Satan has people so messed up they won't care if Muslims tell disbelievers they are wrong about God, but if Muslims dare to say they are wrong about freedom, equality, democracy, economics, laws, morals, entertainment etc then the disbelievers feel threatened and insulted. Truly they don't feel offense if we say the non-Muslims pray the wrong way but they do if we say they play politics incorrectly. That is enough of a sign non-Muslims need a lot of help. If they think it's fine for us to preach something different and in clear contradiction/opposition to their belief about God then by default they have to be fine with us publicly opposing their political, economic and government doctrines and systems. It's either they get offended at us over our belief in God, or about everything Islam teaches, or nothing Islam teaches. Disbelievers are hypocrites if they let us express different beliefs about God but then tell us not to preach Shariah law or denounce their worldly philosophies and revile their unislamic systems and values. All types of Muslims will be extremists from a disbeliever's point of view and vice versa. So anyone who doesn't believe what the prophets taught and doesn't act accordingly is an extremist by default. The correct natural opinion regarding religious beliefs is that if you have the right beliefs then everyone else who believes something different than you, must be an extremist who is wrong and on the road to hell. Although keep in mind I'm talking about beliefs here, not differences of opinion regarding jurisprudence which can validly exist within a religious faith. One logically can never "be okay with someone being a disbeliever as long as they aren't an extreme one". Hence this talk about non-Muslims only fighting extremists, is complete nonsense, by definition every single non-Muslim must view every Muslim as an extremist because Islam/truth is extremely different than falsehood. Disbelievers never champion the orthodoxy of another faith, if they did they wouldn't be disbelievers. So deep within everyone thinks whoever isn't the same religion as them is an extremist, hence everyone preaches to each other trying to eliminate the extremism we believe they have.

At all times one must carefully follow the prophetic methods. No prophet I know of ever started a violent revolution, nor did they use indiscriminate violence in civilian areas, nor did they harm innocents or non-combatants who just happened to be living their lives in ignorance. Likewise no prophet declared war on every country in the world simultaneously. So just because Muslims may be oppressed in many countries, one has to be practical in that the sword is not the answer to all forms of oppression. Diplomacy can work, if it's done correctly. Moses pbuh didn't start a revolution, Jesus pbuh didn't start a revolution, Muhammad pbuh didn't start a revolution. Yet at the same time keep in mind none of them voted in elections and none of them ran for political office or held "inter-faith" dialogues to unite the various religious faiths living in the same localities. The prophetic method is not the revolutionary method, it is not the democratic method, it is not the capitalist method, it is not the machiavellian method and it is not the "Inter-faith" method. It's the pure fundamental Islamic method, as taught to mankind in the Quran and Sunnah which was adhered to by the salaf through sincerity and knowledge. It is definitively not the "moderate Islam" which the disbelievers want and promote. For example most Muslims in the West have a delusion that as a persecuted minority in Mecca the Muslims didn't ruffle any feathers or press for Shariah. Such a notion is entirely false, they got persecuted because they were preaching an entirely different way of life that contradicted, denounced and rejected the status quo and values of the pagan majority who were in power. In public Muhammad pbuh always made his message clear about what his beliefs and goals were even when he couldn't fulfill them and could get in serious harm for expressing his future plans. Muhammad pbuh came with laws from God yet declined the position of leadership of Mecca when it was offered on unislamic terms that included sinfully compromising. Whereas democracy is built upon compromise to secure a majority consensus as if such consensus is sacrosanct due to numbers. God sent Muslims his divine book and it clearly details the answers to the problems we face, the main problem today is that many Muslims do know the answer but they don't know they have the answer or they don't like the answer because it's not the easy/fun answer. Implementing the prophetic plan requires patience, I must mention again.   God never said the right answer to the test of life would be easy or fun or popular or uncontroversial, in fact God explicitly said it would not be, yet it is best for us if we choose and implement the one right answer. What is that 1 right answer to all the problems Muslims have? Well frequently some Muslim preach the pillars of Islam in the name of Islam but the prophets preached Islam in the name of Allah because the 5 pillars are not all there is to Islam. The prophets preached the shahada to the fullest, which at the core fundamental level amounts to 1 meaning, "Total Submission" to the commands and desires of Allah as relayed by his prophets. All prophets taught people they have to become slaves of God. Slavery existed in most of those eras and people knew what a true slave who totally submitted was like in how they thought and lived. Those the prophets preached to knew of slaves who didn't have total submission and they knew of slaves who did. The slaves may have changed the ways they submit to their human masters today, but God's slaves always submit the prophetic way according to the prophetic definition; til death.

Most people will not like to be told even in private that what they are doing is sinful and leads to hell. Many people will tell you to shut up and mind your own business, just like the prophets were told. Yet even if you give in to their demands, to let them sin without suffering reproach, just by personally living according to the law of God they will still label you. This is the hypocrisy of sinners. We don't like people to judge us, but we love to judge others. The bottom line is that by advising people according to the law of God or living the way God wants, they may label you as a crazy radical extremist fanatic. This is because to a crazy person what is right and good seems crazy. What is bad and crazy the insane person sees as good and right. Knowing that the majority of humans will burn in hell, in this world heavily influenced by Satan what is considered "normal" can be crazy in the sight of God. While what is right and good can be considered wrong, stupid or crazy by the majority of people. Whenever God sent a prophet to mankind, the religion they taught was always considered strange by those who rejected it. Since all the prophets were sent by the same God and taught the same religion, anyone who is following the religion of God today would be considered strange. If you are considered "normal" today that means one of two possible things. Either you are very far off the road to paradise and are not practicing the religion of God, or you are living in a special environment where the religion of God is practiced, few environments like this exist in the world. The first is the most likely and the second is very rare. In most societies on earth today, being "normal" is a bad indication. However not being thought of as "normal" doesn't mean you are doing good, you could still be considered strange while being bad. This is because there are different levels of badness and error. Just because someone isn't at an average level of badness, or they aren't in the "normal" type of error that everyone else is, doesn't mean the person is good or following the true religion. A major problem in the world today is the value we place on the opinions of people whether they are good or bad concerning the dead or the living. The only criteria people should be measured up against is the criteria God judges by. Unfortunately Satan has polluted the world thought process so much that the criteria of God tends to be the only thing that people don't care about. Today many ignore judgments made about them done according to the criteria of God, instead paying attention to the judgments people make about them using any other criteria.

This is backwards to how we should be. We should ignore what people say if their opinions are not molded based on the criteria of God and cherish the advisor who tells us to reform ourselves so we can be better in the sight of God. Only God can judge concerning the destination for people in the afterlife. On earth humans can judge each other, but only by the law of God. The judgment of God is always just, whether it's in this life or in the next. There is no problem with the law of God, the problem is with ourselves. God does not ask people to live a lifestyle they are not capable of. God created us and knows we have the ability to obey his laws, he knows our full potential and limitations. God never burdens a person beyond their capacity. If we have a problem with the law of God then we got a problem with God. We don't want to stand on the Day of Judgment as someone who the judge has a problem with. You might have heard the saying before *"it's my house so it's my rules"*, well this is Allah's universe, so you better be living and judging by Allah's rules. If you don't like the law of Allah then you have a simple solution, just go to a universe Allah didn't create, if you stay then you better obey. We will be judged based on our belief and actions. Living in a land ruled by illegitimate governments full of sin may not automatically cast one into the hellfire. Just as living in a land ruled by the law of God won't automatically get one into paradise. It all comes down to us, what do you believe and what do you do? What you believe and do should have nothing to do with what your family, friends, enemies, community or government thinks. The only thing that is important is what God thinks of you. No matter what people do or say to you because of your religious beliefs, or actions done for the sake of God, never be deterred from living how God wants you to and worshipping God. That is the struggle, that is the jihad, that is the test of life, that is the purpose of life, that is the believer's life, that is the way to eternal paradise. May God guide us to the true religion and make us firm, steadfast, grateful and patient with the honor of living and dying as sincere worshippers of the Creator. Why are you concerned about what people may say about your maggoty putrid shell of flesh that is left behind, which has centipedes crawling on your tongue, worms slithering through your nose and spiders scampering across your half-eaten eyeball? Concern yourself with what the angels will say when they extract your soul. Most important of all will be what Allah says when you die. Will your Creator honor and reward you? Will the Creator curse, humiliate and punish you? You will know the answers sooner than you think. The real question is not how Islamic Shariah will fare in the war against Demonic Democracies but about how will Islamic Shariah influence your affair between you and your Maker. The real question is whether you are one of the blessed few who will submit to Islamic Shariah in your personal life beliefs/practices in exchange for eternal paradise and safety from hellfire? Or are you of the 99% of people who will enter the hellfire? The following hadith of Prophet Muhammad pbuh is perhaps the best refutation of a governing system built on the majority opinion/vote. For when it is a prophesied fact that the majority of people will go to hell then clearly the majority opinion is unfit for government.

The sahih (authentic) hadeeth was narrated by al-Bukhaari (6529) from Abu Hurayrah, that the Prophet Muhammad (pbuh) said:

"The first one to be called on the Day of Resurrection will be Adam. He will be shown his progeny and it will be said, 'This is your father Adam.' He will say, 'Here I am at Your service.' He will say: 'Bring forth those who are to be sent to Hell from among your progeny.' He will say, 'O Lord, how many should I bring forth?' He will say, 'Bring forth from every hundred, ninety nine.'" They said: "O Messenger of Allaah, if ninety nine are taken from every hundred of us, what will be left of us?" He said, "My ummah, among the other nations, is like a white hair on a black bull."

Following are some Quranic verses that forbid/prohibit democracy in all its forms including the ancient pagan type and the modern secular and even the Islamisized versions:

Quran 1:5-7

إِيَّاكَ نَعْبُدُ وَإِيَّاكَ نَسْتَعِينُ (٥) اهْدِنَا الصِّرَاطَ الْمُسْتَقِيمَ (٦) صِرَاطَ الَّذِينَ أَنْعَمْتَ عَلَيْهِمْ غَيْرِ الْمَغْضُوبِ عَلَيْهِمْ وَلَا الضَّالِّينَ (٧)

You (Alone) we worship, and You (Alone) we ask for help (for each and everything). (5) Guide us to the Straight Way. (6) The Way of those on whom You have bestowed Your Grace, not (the way) of those who earned Your Anger, nor of those who went astray.(7)

Quran 2:11-13

وَإِذَا قِيلَ لَهُمْ لَا تُفْسِدُوا فِى الْأَرْضِ قَالُوا إِنَّمَا نَحْنُ مُصْلِحُونَ (١١) أَلَا إِنَّهُمْ هُمُ الْمُفْسِدُونَ وَلَكِن لَّا يَشْعُرُونَ (١٢) وَإِذَا قِيلَ لَهُمْ ءَامِنُوا كَمَا ءَامَنَ النَّاسُ قَالُوا أَنُؤْمِنُ كَمَا ءَامَنَ السُّفَهَاءُ أَلَا إِنَّهُمْ هُمُ السُّفَهَاءُ وَلَكِن لَّا يَعْلَمُونَ (١٣)

And when it is said to them: "Make not mischief on the earth," they say: "We are only peacemakers." (11) Verily! They are the ones who make mischief, but they perceive not. (12) And when it is said to them: "Believe as the people (followers of Muhammad, Al-Ansâr and Al-Muhajirûn) have believed," they say: "Shall we believe as the fools have believed?" Verily, they are the fools, but they know not (13)

Quran 2:27

الَّذِينَ يَنقُضُونَ عَهْدَ اللَّهِ مِنْ بَعْدِ مِيثَاقِهِ وَيَقْطَعُونَ مَا أَمَرَ اللَّهُ بِهِ أَن يُوصَلَ وَيُفْسِدُونَ فِى الْأَرْضِ أُوْلَئِكَ هُمُ الْخَاسِرُونَ (٢٧)

Those who break Allâh's Covenant after ratifying it, and sever what Allâh has ordered to be joined (as regards Allâh's religion of Islâmic Monotheism, and to practise its legal laws on the earth and also as regards keeping good relations with kith and kin), and do mischief on earth, it is they who are the losers. (27)

Quran 2:78

وَمِنْهُمْ أُمِّيُّونَ لَا يَعْلَمُونَ الْكِتَابَ إِلَّا أَمَانِىَّ وَإِنْ هُمْ إِلَّا يَظُنُّونَ (٧٨)

And there are among them unlettered people, who know not the Book, but they trust upon false desires and they but guess. (78)

Quran 2:109

وَدَّ كَثِيرٌ مِّنْ أَهْلِ ٱلْكِتَٰبِ لَوْ يَرُدُّونَكُم مِّنْ بَعْدِ إِيمَٰنِكُمْ كُفَّارًا حَسَدًا مِّنْ عِندِ أَنفُسِهِم مِّنْ بَعْدِ مَا تَبَيَّنَ لَهُمُ ٱلْحَقُّ ۖ فَٱعْفُواْ وَٱصْفَحُواْ حَتَّىٰ يَأْتِىَ ٱللَّهُ بِأَمْرِهِۦٓ ۗ إِنَّ ٱللَّهَ عَلَىٰ كُلِّ شَىْءٍ قَدِيرٌ (١٠٩)

Many of the people of the Scripture (Jews and Christians) wish that if they could turn you away as disbelievers after you have believed, out of envy from their ownselves, even after the truth (that Muhammad is Allâh's Messenger) has become manifest unto them. But forgive and overlook, till Allâh brings His Command. Verily, Allâh is Able to do all things. (109)

Quran 2:120-121

وَلَن تَرْضَىٰ عَنكَ ٱلْيَهُودُ وَلَا ٱلنَّصَٰرَىٰ حَتَّىٰ تَتَّبِعَ مِلَّتَهُمْ ۗ قُلْ إِنَّ هُدَى ٱللَّهِ هُوَ ٱلْهُدَىٰ ۗ وَلَئِنِ ٱتَّبَعْتَ أَهْوَآءَهُم بَعْدَ ٱلَّذِى جَآءَكَ مِنَ ٱلْعِلْمِ ۙ مَا لَكَ مِنَ ٱللَّهِ مِن وَلِىٍّ وَلَا نَصِيرٍ (١٢٠) ٱلَّذِينَ ءَاتَيْنَٰهُمُ ٱلْكِتَٰبَ يَتْلُونَهُۥ حَقَّ تِلَاوَتِهِۦٓ أُوْلَٰٓئِكَ يُؤْمِنُونَ بِهِۦ ۗ وَمَن يَكْفُرْ بِهِۦ فَأُوْلَٰٓئِكَ هُمُ ٱلْخَٰسِرُونَ (١٢١)

Never will the Jews nor the Christians be pleased with you till you follow their religion. Say: "Verily, the Guidance of Allâh (i.e. Islâmic Monotheism) that is the (only) Guidance. And if you were to follow their desires after what you have received of Knowledge (i.e. the Qur'ân), then you would have against Allâh neither any Walî (protector or guardian) nor any helper. (120) Those (who embraced Islâm from Banî Israel) to whom We gave the Book [the Taurât (Torah)] [or those (Muhammad's companions) to whom We have given the Book (the Qur'ân)] recite it (i.e. obey its orders and follow its teachings) as it should be recited (i.e. followed), they are the ones that believe therein. And whoso disbelieves in it (the Qur'ân), those are they who are the losers. (121)

Quran 2:124

﴿ وَإِذِ ٱبْتَلَىٰٓ إِبْرَٰهِـۧمَ رَبُّهُۥ بِكَلِمَـٰتٍ فَأَتَمَّهُنَّ ۖ قَالَ إِنِّى جَاعِلُكَ لِلنَّاسِ إِمَامًا ۖ قَالَ وَمِن ذُرِّيَّتِى ۖ قَالَ لَا يَنَالُ عَهْدِى ٱلظَّـٰلِمِينَ (١٢٤)

And (remember) when the Lord of Ibrâhim (Abraham) [i.e., Allâh] tried him with (certain) Commands, which he fulfilled. He (Allâh) said (to him), "Verily, I am going to make you Imam (a leader) for mankind (to follow you)." [Ibrâhim (Abraham)] said, "And of my offspring (to make leaders)." (Allâh) said, "My Covenant (Prophethood) includes not Zâlimûn (polytheists and wrong-doers)." (124)

Quran 2:128-133

رَبَّنَا وَٱجْعَلْنَا مُسْلِمَيْنِ لَكَ وَمِن ذُرِّيَّتِنَآ أُمَّةً مُّسْلِمَةً لَّكَ وَأَرِنَا مَنَاسِكَنَا وَتُبْ عَلَيْنَآ ۖ إِنَّكَ أَنتَ ٱلتَّوَّابُ ٱلرَّحِيمُ (١٢٨) رَبَّنَا وَٱبْعَثْ فِيهِمْ رَسُولًا مِّنْهُمْ يَتْلُوا۟ عَلَيْهِمْ ءَايَـٰتِكَ وَيُعَلِّمُهُمُ ٱلْكِتَـٰبَ وَٱلْحِكْمَةَ وَيُزَكِّيهِمْ ۚ إِنَّكَ أَنتَ ٱلْعَزِيزُ ٱلْحَكِيمُ (١٢٩) وَمَن يَرْغَبُ عَن مِّلَّةِ إِبْرَٰهِـۧمَ إِلَّا مَن سَفِهَ نَفْسَهُۥ ۚ وَلَقَدِ ٱصْطَفَيْنَـٰهُ فِى ٱلدُّنْيَا ۖ وَإِنَّهُۥ فِى ٱلْءَاخِرَةِ لَمِنَ ٱلصَّـٰلِحِينَ (١٣٠) إِذْ قَالَ لَهُۥ رَبُّهُۥٓ أَسْلِمْ ۖ قَالَ أَسْلَمْتُ لِرَبِّ ٱلْعَـٰلَمِينَ (١٣١) وَوَصَّىٰ بِهَآ إِبْرَٰهِـۧمُ بَنِيهِ وَيَعْقُوبُ يَـٰبَنِىَّ إِنَّ ٱللَّهَ ٱصْطَفَىٰ لَكُمُ ٱلدِّينَ فَلَا تَمُوتُنَّ إِلَّا وَأَنتُم مُّسْلِمُونَ (١٣٢) أَمْ كُنتُمْ شُهَدَآءَ إِذْ حَضَرَ يَعْقُوبَ ٱلْمَوْتُ إِذْ قَالَ لِبَنِيهِ مَا تَعْبُدُونَ مِنۢ بَعْدِى قَالُوا۟ نَعْبُدُ إِلَـٰهَكَ وَإِلَـٰهَ ءَابَآئِكَ إِبْرَٰهِـۧمَ وَإِسْمَـٰعِيلَ وَإِسْحَـٰقَ إِلَـٰهًا وَٰحِدًا وَنَحْنُ لَهُۥ مُسْلِمُونَ (١٣٣)

"Our Lord! And make us submissive unto You and of our offspring a nation submissive unto You, and show us our Manâsik (all the ceremonies of pilgrimage - Hajj and 'Umrah), and accept our repentance. Truly, You are the One Who accepts repentance, the Most Merciful. (128) "Our Lord! Send amongst them a Messenger of their own (and indeed Allâh answered their invocation by sending Muhammad), who shall recite unto them Your Verses and instruct them in the Book (this Qur'ân) and Al-Hikmah (full knowledge of the Islâmic laws and jurisprudence or wisdom or Prophethood), and purify them. Verily! You are the All-Mighty, the All-Wise." (129) And who turns away from the religion of Ibrâhim (Abraham) (i.e. Islâmic Monotheism) except him who befools himself? Truly, We chose him in this world and verily, in the Hereafter he will be among the righteous. (130) When his Lord said to him, "Submit (i.e. be a Muslim)!" He said, "I have submitted myself (as a Muslim) to the Lord of the

'Alamîn (mankind, jinn and all that exists)." (131) And this (submission to Allâh, Islâm) was enjoined by Ibrâhim (Abraham) upon his sons and by Ya'qûb (Jacob), (saying), "O my sons! Allâh has chosen for you the (true) religion, then die not except in the Faith of Islâm (as Muslims - Islâmic Monotheism)." (132) Or were you witnesses when death approached Ya'qûb (Jacob)? When he said unto his sons, "What will you worship after me?" They said, "We shall worship your Ilâh (God - Allâh), the Ilâh (God) of your fathers, Ibrâhim (Abraham), Ismâ'il (Ishmael), Ishâq (Isaac), One Ilâh (God), and to Him we submit (in Islâm)." (133)

Quran 2:137-138

فَإِنْ ءَامَنُواْ بِمِثْلِ مَا ءَامَنتُم بِهِۦ فَقَدِ ٱهْتَدَواْ وَإِن تَوَلَّوْاْ فَإِنَّمَا هُمْ فِى شِقَاقٍ فَسَيَكْفِيكَهُمُ ٱللَّهُ وَهُوَ ٱلسَّمِيعُ ٱلْعَلِيمُ (١٣٧) صِبْغَةَ ٱللَّهِ وَمَنْ أَحْسَنُ مِنَ ٱللَّهِ صِبْغَةً وَنَحْنُ لَهُۥ عَٰبِدُونَ (١٣٨)

So if they believe in the like of that which you believe, then they are rightly guided, but if they turn away, then they are only in opposition. So Allâh will suffice for you against them. And He is the All-Hearer, the All-Knower. (137) [Our Sibghah (religion) is] the Sibghah (Religion) of Allâh (Islâm) and which Sibghah (religion) can be better than Allâh's? And we are His worshippers. (138)

Quran 2:213

كَانَ ٱلنَّاسُ أُمَّةً وَٰحِدَةً فَبَعَثَ ٱللَّهُ ٱلنَّبِيِّۦنَ مُبَشِّرِينَ وَمُنذِرِينَ وَأَنزَلَ مَعَهُمُ ٱلْكِتَٰبَ بِٱلْحَقِّ لِيَحْكُمَ بَيْنَ ٱلنَّاسِ فِيمَا ٱخْتَلَفُواْ فِيهِ وَمَا ٱخْتَلَفَ فِيهِ إِلَّا ٱلَّذِينَ أُوتُوهُ مِنۢ بَعْدِ مَا جَاءَتْهُمُ ٱلْبَيِّنَٰتُ بَغْيًۢا بَيْنَهُمْ فَهَدَى ٱللَّهُ ٱلَّذِينَ ءَامَنُواْ لِمَا ٱخْتَلَفُواْ فِيهِ مِنَ ٱلْحَقِّ بِإِذْنِهِۦ وَٱللَّهُ يَهْدِى مَن يَشَاءُ إِلَىٰ صِرَٰطٍ مُّسْتَقِيمٍ (٢١٣)

Mankind were one community and Allâh sent Prophets with glad tidings and warnings, and with them He sent the Scripture in truth to judge between people in matters wherein they differed. And only those to whom (the Scripture) was given differed concerning it after clear proofs had come unto them through hatred, one to another. Then Allâh by His Leave guided those who believed to the truth of that wherein they differed. And Allâh guides whom He wills to a Straight Path. (213)

Quran 2:246-247

أَلَمْ تَرَ إِلَى ٱلْمَلَإِ مِنْ بَنِىٓ إِسْرَٰٓءِيلَ مِنْ بَعْدِ مُوسَىٰٓ إِذْ قَالُوا۟ لِنَبِىٍّ لَّهُمُ ٱبْعَثْ لَنَا مَلِكًا نُّقَٰتِلْ فِى سَبِيلِ ٱللَّهِ قَالَ هَلْ عَسَيْتُمْ إِن كُتِبَ عَلَيْكُمُ ٱلْقِتَالُ أَلَّا تُقَٰتِلُوا۟ قَالُوا۟ وَمَا لَنَآ أَلَّا نُقَٰتِلَ فِى سَبِيلِ ٱللَّهِ وَقَدْ أُخْرِجْنَا مِن دِيَٰرِنَا وَأَبْنَآئِنَا فَلَمَّا كُتِبَ عَلَيْهِمُ ٱلْقِتَالُ تَوَلَّوْا۟ إِلَّا قَلِيلًا مِّنْهُمْ وَٱللَّهُ عَلِيمٌۢ بِٱلظَّٰلِمِينَ (٢٤٦) وَقَالَ لَهُمْ نَبِيُّهُمْ إِنَّ ٱللَّهَ قَدْ بَعَثَ لَكُمْ طَالُوتَ مَلِكًا قَالُوٓا۟ أَنَّىٰ يَكُونُ لَهُ ٱلْمُلْكُ عَلَيْنَا وَنَحْنُ أَحَقُّ بِٱلْمُلْكِ مِنْهُ وَلَمْ يُؤْتَ سَعَةً مِّنَ ٱلْمَالِ قَالَ إِنَّ ٱللَّهَ ٱصْطَفَىٰهُ عَلَيْكُمْ وَزَادَهُۥ بَسْطَةً فِى ٱلْعِلْمِ وَٱلْجِسْمِ وَٱللَّهُ يُؤْتِى مُلْكَهُۥ مَن يَشَآءُ وَٱللَّهُ وَٰسِعٌ عَلِيمٌ (٢٤٧)

Have you not thought about the group of the Children of Israel after (the time of) Musâ (Moses)? When they said to a Prophet of theirs, "Appoint for us a king and we will fight in Allâh's Way." He said, "Would you then refrain from fighting, if fighting was prescribed for you?" They said, "Why should we not fight in Allâh's Way while we have been driven out of our homes and our children (families have been taken as captives)?" But when fighting was ordered for them, they turned away, all except a few of them. And Allâh is All-Aware of the Zâlimûn (polytheists and wrong-doers). (246) And their Prophet (Samuel) said to them, "Indeed Allâh has appointed Talût (Saul) as a king over you." They said, "How can he be a king over us when we are fitter than him for the kingdom, and he has not been given enough wealth." He said: "Verily, Allâh has chosen him above you and has increased him abundantly in knowledge and stature. And Allâh grants His Kingdom to whom He wills. And Allâh is All-Sufficient for His creatures' needs, All-Knower." (247)

Quran 2:249-253

فَلَمَّا فَصَلَ طَالُوتُ بِٱلْجُنُودِ قَالَ إِنَّ ٱللَّهَ مُبْتَلِيكُم بِنَهَرٍ فَمَن شَرِبَ مِنْهُ فَلَيْسَ مِنِّى وَمَن لَّمْ يَطْعَمْهُ فَإِنَّهُۥ مِنِّىٓ إِلَّا مَنِ ٱغْتَرَفَ غُرْفَةًۢ بِيَدِهِۦ فَشَرِبُوا۟ مِنْهُ إِلَّا قَلِيلًا مِّنْهُمْ فَلَمَّا جَاوَزَهُۥ هُوَ وَٱلَّذِينَ ءَامَنُوا۟ مَعَهُۥ قَالُوا۟ لَا طَاقَةَ لَنَا ٱلْيَوْمَ بِجَالُوتَ وَجُنُودِهِۦ قَالَ ٱلَّذِينَ يَظُنُّونَ أَنَّهُم مُّلَٰقُوا۟ ٱللَّهِ كَم مِّن فِئَةٍ قَلِيلَةٍ غَلَبَتْ فِئَةً كَثِيرَةًۢ بِإِذْنِ ٱللَّهِ وَٱللَّهُ مَعَ ٱلصَّٰبِرِينَ (٢٤٩) وَلَمَّا بَرَزُوا۟ لِجَالُوتَ وَجُنُودِهِۦ قَالُوا۟ رَبَّنَآ أَفْرِغْ عَلَيْنَا صَبْرًا وَثَبِّتْ أَقْدَامَنَا وَٱنصُرْنَا عَلَى ٱلْقَوْمِ ٱلْكَٰفِرِينَ (٢٥٠) فَهَزَمُوهُم بِإِذْنِ ٱللَّهِ وَقَتَلَ دَاوُۥدُ جَالُوتَ وَءَاتَىٰهُ ٱللَّهُ ٱلْمُلْكَ وَٱلْحِكْمَةَ وَعَلَّمَهُۥ مِمَّا يَشَآءُ وَلَوْلَا دَفْعُ ٱللَّهِ ٱلنَّاسَ بَعْضَهُم

بِبَعْضٍ لَّفَسَدَتِ ٱلْأَرْضُ وَلَـٰكِنَّ ٱللَّهَ ذُو فَضْلٍ عَلَى ٱلْعَـٰلَمِينَ (٢٥١) تِلْكَ ءَايَـٰتُ ٱللَّهِ نَتْلُوهَا عَلَيْكَ بِٱلْحَقِّ وَإِنَّكَ لَمِنَ ٱلْمُرْسَلِينَ (٢٥٢) ۞ تِلْكَ ٱلرُّسُلُ فَضَّلْنَا بَعْضَهُمْ عَلَىٰ بَعْضٍ مِّنْهُم مَّن كَلَّمَ ٱللَّهُ وَرَفَعَ بَعْضَهُمْ دَرَجَـٰتٍ وَءَاتَيْنَا عِيسَى ٱبْنَ مَرْيَمَ ٱلْبَيِّنَـٰتِ وَأَيَّدْنَـٰهُ بِرُوحِ ٱلْقُدُسِ وَلَوْ شَآءَ ٱللَّهُ مَا ٱقْتَتَلَ ٱلَّذِينَ مِنۢ بَعْدِهِم مِّنۢ بَعْدِ مَا جَآءَتْهُمُ ٱلْبَيِّنَـٰتُ وَلَـٰكِنِ ٱخْتَلَفُوا۟ فَمِنْهُم مَّنْ ءَامَنَ وَمِنْهُم مَّن كَفَرَ وَلَوْ شَآءَ ٱللَّهُ مَا ٱقْتَتَلُوا۟ وَلَـٰكِنَّ ٱللَّهَ يَفْعَلُ مَا يُرِيدُ (٢٥٣)

Then when Tâlût (Saul) set out with the army, he said: "Verily! Allâh will try you by a river. So whoever drinks thereof, he is not of me, and whoever tastes it not, he is of me, except him who takes (thereof) in the hollow of his hand." Yet, they drank thereof, all, except a few of them. So when he had crossed it (the river), he and those who believed with him, they said: "We have no power this day against Jâlût (Goliath) and his hosts." But those who knew with certainty that they were to meet their Lord, said: "How often a small group overcame a mighty host by Allâh's Leave?" And Allâh is with As-Sâbirûn (the patient). (249) And when they advanced to meet Jâlût (Goliath) and his forces, they invoked: "Our Lord! Pour forth on us patience, and set firm our feet and make us victorious over the disbelieving people." (250) So they routed them by Allâh's Leave and Dâwûd (David) killed Jâlût (Goliath), and Allâh gave him [Dawûd (David)] the kingdom [after the death of Talût (Saul) and Samuel] and Al¬Hikmah (Prophethood), and taught him of that which He willed. And if Allâh did not check one set of people by means of another, the earth would indeed be full of mischief. But Allâh is full of Bounty to the 'Alamîn (mankind, jinn and all that exists). (251) These are the Verses of Allâh, We recite them to you (O Muhammad) in truth, and surely, you are one of the Messengers (of Allâh). (252) Those Messengers! We preferred some often to others; to some of them Allâh spoke (directly); others He raised to degrees (of honour); and to 'Īsā (Jesus), the son of Maryam (Mary), We gave clear proofs and evidences, and supported him with Rûh-ul-Qudus [Jibrael (Gabriel)]. If Allâh had willed, succeeding generations would not have fought against each other, after clear Verses of Allâh had come to them, but they differed - some of them believed and others disbelieved. If Allâh had willed, they would not have fought against one another, but Allâh does what He likes. (253)

Quran 2:256-257

لَا إِكْرَاهَ فِى ٱلدِّينِ قَد تَّبَيَّنَ ٱلرُّشْدُ مِنَ ٱلْغَىِّ فَمَن يَكْفُرْ بِٱلطَّـٰغُوتِ وَيُؤْمِنۢ بِٱللَّهِ فَقَدِ ٱسْتَمْسَكَ بِٱلْعُرْوَةِ ٱلْوُثْقَىٰ لَا ٱنفِصَامَ لَهَا وَٱللَّهُ سَمِيعٌ عَلِيمٌ (٢٥٦) ٱللَّهُ وَلِىُّ ٱلَّذِينَ ءَامَنُوا۟ يُخْرِجُهُم مِّنَ ٱلظُّلُمَـٰتِ إِلَى ٱلنُّورِ وَٱلَّذِينَ كَفَرُوٓا۟ أَوْلِيَآؤُهُمُ ٱلطَّـٰغُوتُ يُخْرِجُونَهُم مِّنَ ٱلنُّورِ إِلَى ٱلظُّلُمَـٰتِ أُو۟لَـٰٓئِكَ أَصْحَـٰبُ ٱلنَّارِ هُمْ فِيهَا خَـٰلِدُونَ (٢٥٧)

There is no compulsion in religion. Verily, the Right Path has become distinct from the wrong path. Whoever disbelieves in Tâghût [false deities, false leaders, false judges] and believes in Allâh, then he has grasped the most trustworthy handhold that will never break. And Allâh is All-Hearer, All-Knower. (256) Allâh is the Walî (Protector or Guardian) of those who believe. He brings them out from darkness into light. But as for those who disbelieve, their Auliyâ (supporters and helpers) are Tâghût [false deities and false leaders], they bring them out from light into darkness. Those are the dwellers of the Fire, and they will abide therein forever. (257)

Quran 3:3-4

نَزَّلَ عَلَيْكَ ٱلْكِتَـٰبَ بِٱلْحَقِّ مُصَدِّقًا لِّمَا بَيْنَ يَدَيْهِ وَأَنزَلَ ٱلتَّوْرَىٰةَ وَٱلْإِنجِيلَ (٣) مِن قَبْلُ هُدًى لِّلنَّاسِ وَأَنزَلَ ٱلْفُرْقَانَ إِنَّ ٱلَّذِينَ كَفَرُوا۟ بِـَٔايَـٰتِ ٱللَّهِ لَهُمْ عَذَابٌ شَدِيدٌ وَٱللَّهُ عَزِيزٌ ذُو ٱنتِقَامٍ (٤)

It is He Who has sent down the Book (the Qur'ân) to you (Muhammad) with truth, confirming what came before it. And he sent down the Taurât (Torah) and the Injeel (3) Aforetime, as a guidance to mankind, And He sent down the criterion [of judgement between right and wrong (this Qur'ân)]. Truly, those who disbelieve in the Ayât (proofs, evidences, verses, lessons, signs, revelations, etc.) of Allâh, for them there is a severe torment; and Allâh is All-Mighty, All-Able of Retribution. (4)

Quran 3:19-23

إِنَّ ٱلدِّينَ عِندَ ٱللَّهِ ٱلْإِسْلَـٰمُ وَمَا ٱخْتَلَفَ ٱلَّذِينَ أُوتُوا۟ ٱلْكِتَـٰبَ إِلَّا مِنۢ بَعْدِ مَا جَآءَهُمُ ٱلْعِلْمُ بَغْيًۢا بَيْنَهُمْ وَمَن يَكْفُرْ بِـَٔايَـٰتِ ٱللَّهِ فَإِنَّ ٱللَّهَ سَرِيعُ ٱلْحِسَابِ (١٩) فَإِنْ حَآجُّوكَ فَقُلْ أَسْلَمْتُ وَجْهِىَ لِلَّهِ وَمَنِ ٱتَّبَعَنِ وَقُل لِّلَّذِينَ أُوتُوا۟ ٱلْكِتَـٰبَ وَٱلْأُمِّيِّـۧنَ ءَأَسْلَمْتُمْ فَإِنْ أَسْلَمُوا۟

فَقَدِ ٱهْتَدَوا وَإِن تَوَلَّوْا فَإِنَّمَا عَلَيْكَ ٱلْبَلَٰغُ وَٱللَّهُ بَصِيرٌ بِٱلْعِبَادِ (٢٠) إِنَّ ٱلَّذِينَ يَكْفُرُونَ بِـَٔايَٰتِ ٱللَّهِ وَيَقْتُلُونَ ٱلنَّبِيِّـۧنَ بِغَيْرِ حَقٍّ وَيَقْتُلُونَ ٱلَّذِينَ يَأْمُرُونَ بِٱلْقِسْطِ مِنَ ٱلنَّاسِ فَبَشِّرْهُم بِعَذَابٍ أَلِيمٍ (٢١) أُوْلَٰٓئِكَ ٱلَّذِينَ حَبِطَتْ أَعْمَٰلُهُمْ فِى ٱلدُّنْيَا وَٱلْءَاخِرَةِ وَمَا لَهُم مِّن نَّٰصِرِينَ (٢٢) أَلَمْ تَرَ إِلَى ٱلَّذِينَ أُوتُوا نَصِيبًا مِّنَ ٱلْكِتَٰبِ يُدْعَوْنَ إِلَىٰ كِتَٰبِ ٱللَّهِ لِيَحْكُمَ بَيْنَهُمْ ثُمَّ يَتَوَلَّىٰ فَرِيقٌ مِّنْهُمْ وَهُم مُّعْرِضُونَ (٢٣)

Truly, the religion with Allâh is Islâm. Those who were given the Scripture (Jews and Christians) did not differ except, out of mutual jealousy, after knowledge had come to them. And whoever disbelieves in the Ayât (proofs, evidences, verses, signs, revelations, etc.) of Allâh, then surely, Allâh is Swift in calling to account. (19) So if they dispute with you (Muhammad) say: "I have submitted myself to Allâh (in Islâm), and (so have) those who follow me." And say to those who were given the Scripture (Jews and Christians) and to those who are illiterates (Arab pagans): "Do you (also) submit yourselves (to Allâh in Islâm)?" If they do, they are rightly guided; but if they turn away, your duty is only to convey the Message; and Allâh is All-Seer of (His) slaves(20) Verily! Those who disbelieve in the Ayât (proofs, evidences, verses, lessons, signs, revelations, etc.) of Allâh and kill the Prophets without right, and kill those men who order just dealings, ... then announce to them a painful torment. (21) They are those whose works will be lost in this world and in the Hereafter, and they will have no helpers. (22) Have you not seen those who have been given a portion of the Scripture? They are being invited to the Book of Allâh to settle their dispute, then a party of them turn away, and they are averse. (23)

Quran 3:26

قُلِ ٱللَّهُمَّ مَٰلِكَ ٱلْمُلْكِ تُؤْتِى ٱلْمُلْكَ مَن تَشَآءُ وَتَنزِعُ ٱلْمُلْكَ مِمَّن تَشَآءُ وَتُعِزُّ مَن تَشَآءُ وَتُذِلُّ مَن تَشَآءُ بِيَدِكَ ٱلْخَيْرُ إِنَّكَ عَلَىٰ كُلِّ شَىْءٍ قَدِيرٌ (٢٦)

Say (O Muhammad): "O Allâh! Possessor of the kingdom, You give the kingdom to whom You will, and You take the kingdom from whom You will, and You endue with honour whom You will, and You humiliate whom You will. In Your Hand is the good. Verily, You are Able to do all things. (26)

Quran 3:31-32

قُلْ إِن كُنتُمْ تُحِبُّونَ ٱللَّهَ فَٱتَّبِعُونِى يُحْبِبْكُمُ ٱللَّهُ وَيَغْفِرْ لَكُمْ ذُنُوبَكُمْ وَٱللَّهُ غَفُورٌ رَّحِيمٌ
(٣١) قُلْ أَطِيعُواْ ٱللَّهَ وَٱلرَّسُولَ فَإِن تَوَلَّوْاْ فَإِنَّ ٱللَّهَ لَا يُحِبُّ ٱلْكَـٰفِرِينَ (٣٢)

Say (O Muhammad to mankind): "If you (really) love Allâh then follow me (i.e. accept Islâmic Monotheism, follow the Qur'ân and the Sunnah), Allâh will love you and forgive you your sins. And Allâh is Oft-Forgiving, Most Merciful." (31) Say: "Obey Allâh and the Messenger (Muhammad)." But if they turn away, then Allâh does not like the disbelievers (32)

Quran 3:81-85

وَإِذْ أَخَذَ ٱللَّهُ مِيثَـٰقَ ٱلنَّبِيِّـۧنَ لَمَآ ءَاتَيْتُكُم مِّن كِتَـٰبٍ وَحِكْمَةٍ ثُمَّ جَآءَكُمْ رَسُولٌ مُّصَدِّقٌ
لِّمَا مَعَكُمْ لَتُؤْمِنُنَّ بِهِۦ وَلَتَنصُرُنَّهُۥ قَالَ ءَأَقْرَرْتُمْ وَأَخَذْتُمْ عَلَىٰ ذَٰلِكُمْ إِصْرِى قَالُوٓاْ
أَقْرَرْنَا قَالَ فَٱشْهَدُواْ وَأَنَا۠ مَعَكُم مِّنَ ٱلشَّـٰهِدِينَ (٨١) فَمَن تَوَلَّىٰ بَعْدَ ذَٰلِكَ فَأُوْلَـٰٓئِكَ هُمُ
ٱلْفَـٰسِقُونَ (٨٢) أَفَغَيْرَ دِينِ ٱللَّهِ يَبْغُونَ وَلَهُۥٓ أَسْلَمَ مَن فِى ٱلسَّمَـٰوَٰتِ وَٱلْأَرْضِ طَوْعًا
وَكَرْهًا وَإِلَيْهِ يُرْجَعُونَ (٨٣) قُلْ ءَامَنَّا بِٱللَّهِ وَمَآ أُنزِلَ عَلَيْنَا وَمَآ أُنزِلَ عَلَىٰٓ إِبْرَٰهِيمَ
وَإِسْمَـٰعِيلَ وَإِسْحَـٰقَ وَيَعْقُوبَ وَٱلْأَسْبَاطِ وَمَآ أُوتِىَ مُوسَىٰ وَعِيسَىٰ وَٱلنَّبِيُّونَ مِن رَّبِّهِمْ
لَا نُفَرِّقُ بَيْنَ أَحَدٍ مِّنْهُمْ وَنَحْنُ لَهُۥ مُسْلِمُونَ (٨٤) وَمَن يَبْتَغِ غَيْرَ ٱلْإِسْلَـٰمِ دِينًا فَلَن
يُقْبَلَ مِنْهُ وَهُوَ فِى ٱلْأَخِرَةِ مِنَ ٱلْخَـٰسِرِينَ (٨٥)

And (remember) when Allâh took the Covenant of the Prophets, saying: "Take whatever I gave you from the Book and Hikmah (understanding of the Laws of Allâh), and afterwards there will come to you a Messenger (Muhammad) confirming what is with you; you must, then, believe in him and help him." Allâh said: "Do you agree (to it) and will you take up My Covenant (which I conclude with you)?" They said: "We agree." He said: "Then bear witness; and I am with you among the witnesses (for this)." (81) Then whoever turns away after this, they are the Fâsiqûn (rebellious: those who turn away from Allâh's Obedience). (82) Do they seek other than the religion of Allâh (the true Islâmic Monotheism worshipping none but Allâh Alone), while to Him submitted all creatures in the heavens and the earth, willingly or unwillingly. And to Him shall they all be returned. (83) Say (O Muhammad): "We believe in Allâh and in what has been sent down to us, and what was sent down to Ibrâhim (Abraham), Ismâ'il (Ishmael), Ishâq (Isaac), Ya'qûb (Jacob) and Al-Asbât [the offspring twelve sons of Ya'qûb (Jacob)] and what was given to Mûsa (Moses), 'Īsā (Jesus) and the Prophets from their Lord. We make no distinction between one another among them and to Him (Allâh) we have submitted (in Islâm)." (84) And whoever seeks a religion other than Islâm, it will never be accepted of him, and in the Hereafter he will be one of the losers. (85)

Quran 3:90-106

قُلْ يَـٰٓأَهْلَ ٱلْكِتَـٰبِ لِمَ تَصُدُّونَ عَن سَبِيلِ ٱللَّهِ مَنْ ءَامَنَ تَبْغُونَهَا عِوَجًا وَأَنتُمْ شُهَدَآءُ وَمَا ٱللَّهُ بِغَـٰفِلٍ عَمَّا تَعْمَلُونَ (٩٩) يَـٰٓأَيُّهَا ٱلَّذِينَ ءَامَنُوٓا۟ إِن تُطِيعُوا۟ فَرِيقًا مِّنَ ٱلَّذِينَ أُوتُوا۟ ٱلْكِتَـٰبَ يَرُدُّوكُم بَعْدَ إِيمَـٰنِكُمْ كَـٰفِرِينَ (١٠٠) وَكَيْفَ تَكْفُرُونَ وَأَنتُمْ تُتْلَىٰ عَلَيْكُمْ ءَايَـٰتُ ٱللَّهِ وَفِيكُمْ رَسُولُهُۥ وَمَن يَعْتَصِم بِٱللَّهِ فَقَدْ هُدِىَ إِلَىٰ صِرَٰطٍ مُّسْتَقِيمٍ (١٠١) يَـٰٓأَيُّهَا ٱلَّذِينَ ءَامَنُوا۟ ٱتَّقُوا۟ ٱللَّهَ حَقَّ تُقَاتِهِۦ وَلَا تَمُوتُنَّ إِلَّا وَأَنتُم مُّسْلِمُونَ (١٠٢) وَٱعْتَصِمُوا۟ بِحَبْلِ ٱللَّهِ جَمِيعًا وَلَا تَفَرَّقُوا۟ وَٱذْكُرُوا۟ نِعْمَتَ ٱللَّهِ عَلَيْكُمْ إِذْ كُنتُمْ أَعْدَآءً فَأَلَّفَ بَيْنَ قُلُوبِكُمْ فَأَصْبَحْتُم بِنِعْمَتِهِۦٓ إِخْوَٰنًا وَكُنتُمْ عَلَىٰ شَفَا حُفْرَةٍ مِّنَ ٱلنَّارِ فَأَنقَذَكُم مِّنْهَا كَذَٰلِكَ يُبَيِّنُ ٱللَّهُ لَكُمْ ءَايَـٰتِهِۦ لَعَلَّكُمْ تَهْتَدُونَ (١٠٣) وَلْتَكُن مِّنكُمْ أُمَّةٌ يَدْعُونَ إِلَى ٱلْخَيْرِ وَيَأْمُرُونَ بِٱلْمَعْرُوفِ وَيَنْهَوْنَ عَنِ ٱلْمُنكَرِ وَأُو۟لَـٰٓئِكَ هُمُ ٱلْمُفْلِحُونَ (١٠٤) وَلَا تَكُونُوا۟ كَٱلَّذِينَ تَفَرَّقُوا۟ وَٱخْتَلَفُوا۟ مِنْ بَعْدِ مَا جَآءَهُمُ ٱلْبَيِّنَـٰتُ وَأُو۟لَـٰٓئِكَ لَهُمْ عَذَابٌ عَظِيمٌ (١٠٥) يَوْمَ تَبْيَضُّ وُجُوهٌ وَتَسْوَدُّ وُجُوهٌ فَأَمَّا ٱلَّذِينَ ٱسْوَدَّتْ وُجُوهُهُمْ أَكَفَرْتُم بَعْدَ إِيمَـٰنِكُمْ فَذُوقُوا۟ ٱلْعَذَابَ بِمَا كُنتُمْ تَكْفُرُونَ (١٠٦)

Say: "O people of the Scripture (Jews and Christians)! Why do you stop those who have believed, from the Path of Allâh, seeking to make it seem crooked, while you (yourselves) are witnesses [to Muhammad as a Messenger of Allâh and Islâm (Allâh's Religion, i.e. to worship none but Him Alone)]? And Allâh is not unaware of what you do." (99) O you who believe! If you obey a group of those who were given the Scripture (Jews and Christians), they would (indeed) render you disbelievers after you have believed! (100) And how would you disbelieve, while unto you are recited the Verses of Allâh, and among you is His Messenger (Muhammad)? And whoever holds firmly to Allâh, (i.e. follows Islâm — Allâh's Religion, and obeys all that Allâh has ordered, practically), then he is indeed guided to a Right Path. (101) O you who believe! Fear Allâh (by doing all that He has ordered and by abstaining from all that He has forbidden) as He should be feared. [Obey Him, be thankful to Him, and remember Him always], and die not except in a state of Islâm [as Muslims (with complete submission to Allâh)]. (102) And hold fast, all of you together, to the Rope of Allâh (i.e. this Qur'ân), and be not divided among yourselves, and remember Allâh's Favour on you, for you were enemies one to another but He joined your hearts together, so that, by His Grace, you became brethren (in Islâmic Faith), and you were on the brink of a pit of Fire, and He saved you from it. Thus Allâh makes His Ayât (proofs, evidences, verses, lessons, signs, revelations, etc.,) clear to you, that you may be guided. (103) Let there arise out of you a group of people inviting to all that is good (Islâm), enjoining Al-Ma'rûf (i.e. Islâmic Monotheism and all that Islâm orders one to do) and forbidding Al-Munkar (polytheism and disbelief and all that Islâm has forbidden). And it is they who are the successful. (104) And be not as those who divided and differed among themselves after the clear proofs had come to them. It is they for whom there is an awful torment. (105) On the Day (i.e. the Day of Resurrection) when some faces will become white and some faces will become black; as for those whose faces will become black (to them will be said): "Did you reject Faith after accepting it? Then taste the torment (in Hell) for rejecting Faith." (106)

Quran 3:110-112

كُنتُمْ خَيْرَ أُمَّةٍ أُخْرِجَتْ لِلنَّاسِ تَأْمُرُونَ بِالْمَعْرُوفِ وَتَنْهَوْنَ عَنِ ٱلْمُنكَرِ وَتُؤْمِنُونَ بِٱللَّهِ وَلَوْ ءَامَنَ أَهْلُ ٱلْكِتَٰبِ لَكَانَ خَيْرًا لَّهُم مِّنْهُمُ ٱلْمُؤْمِنُونَ وَأَكْثَرُهُمُ ٱلْفَٰسِقُونَ (١١٠) لَن يَضُرُّوكُمْ إِلَّا أَذًى وَإِن يُقَٰتِلُوكُمْ يُوَلُّوكُمُ ٱلْأَدْبَارَ ثُمَّ لَا يُنصَرُونَ (١١١) ضُرِبَتْ عَلَيْهِمُ ٱلذِّلَّةُ أَيْنَ مَا ثُقِفُوٓا۟ إِلَّا بِحَبْلٍ مِّنَ ٱللَّهِ وَحَبْلٍ مِّنَ ٱلنَّاسِ وَبَآءُو بِغَضَبٍ مِّنَ ٱللَّهِ وَضُرِبَتْ عَلَيْهِمُ ٱلْمَسْكَنَةُ ذَٰلِكَ بِأَنَّهُمْ كَانُوا۟ يَكْفُرُونَ بِـَٔايَٰتِ ٱللَّهِ وَيَقْتُلُونَ ٱلْأَنۢبِيَآءَ بِغَيْرِ حَقٍّ ذَٰلِكَ بِمَا عَصَوا۟ وَّكَانُوا۟ يَعْتَدُونَ (١١٢)

You [true believers in Islâmic Monotheism, and real followers of Prophet Muhammad and his Sunnah] are the best of peoples ever raised up for mankind; you enjoin Al-Ma'rûf (i.e. Islâmic Monotheism and all that Islâm has ordained) and forbid Al-Munkar (polytheism, disbelief and all that Islâm has forbidden), and you believe in Allâh. And had the people of the Scripture (Jews and Christians) believed, it would have been better for them; among them are some who have faith, but most of them are Al-Fâsiqûn (disobedient to Allâh - and rebellious against Allâh's Command). (110) They will do you no harm, barring a trifling annoyance; and if they fight against you, they will show you their backs, and they will not be helped. (111) Indignity is put over them wherever they may be, except when under a covenant (of protection) from Allâh, and from men; they have drawn on themselves the Wrath of Allâh, and destruction is put over them. This is because they disbelieved in the Ayât (proofs, evidences, verses, lessons, signs, revelations, etc.) of Allâh and killed the Prophets without right. This is because they disobeyed (Allâh) and used to transgress beyond bounds (in Allâh's disobedience, crimes and sins). (112)

Quran 3:118

يَـٰٓأَيُّهَا ٱلَّذِينَ ءَامَنُوا۟ لَا تَتَّخِذُوا۟ بِطَانَةً مِّن دُونِكُمْ لَا يَأْلُونَكُمْ خَبَالًا وَدُّوا۟ مَا عَنِتُّمْ قَدْ بَدَتِ ٱلْبَغْضَاءُ مِنْ أَفْوَاهِهِمْ وَمَا تُخْفِى صُدُورُهُمْ أَكْبَرُ قَدْ بَيَّنَّا لَكُمُ ٱلْءَايَـٰتِ إِن كُنتُمْ تَعْقِلُونَ (١١٨)

O you who believe! Take not as (your) Bitânah (advisors, consultants, protectors, helpers, friends) those outside your religion (pagans, Jews, Christians, and hypocrites) since they will not fail to do their best to corrupt you. They desire to harm you severely. Hatred has already appeared from their mouths, but what their breasts conceal is far worse. Indeed We have made plain to you the Ayât (proofs, evidences, verses) if you understand. (118)

Quran 3:137-139

قَدْ خَلَتْ مِن قَبْلِكُمْ سُنَنٌ فَسِيرُوا۟ فِى ٱلْأَرْضِ فَٱنظُرُوا۟ كَيْفَ كَانَ عَـٰقِبَةُ ٱلْمُكَذِّبِينَ (١٣٧) هَـٰذَا بَيَانٌ لِّلنَّاسِ وَهُدًى وَمَوْعِظَةٌ لِّلْمُتَّقِينَ (١٣٨) وَلَا تَهِنُوا۟ وَلَا تَحْزَنُوا۟ وَأَنتُمُ ٱلْأَعْلَوْنَ إِن كُنتُم مُّؤْمِنِينَ (١٣٩)

Many similar ways (and mishaps of life) were faced by nations (believers and disbelievers) that have passed away before you, so travel through the earth, and see what was the end of those who disbelieved (in the Oneness *of Allâh, and disobeyed Him and His Messengers). (137) This (the Qur'ân) is a plain statement for mankind, a guidance and instruction to those who are Al-Muttaqûn (the pious). (138) So do not become weak (against your enemy), nor be sad, and you will be superior (in victory) if you are indeed (true) believers. (139)*

Quran 3:144

وَمَا مُحَمَّدٌ إِلَّا رَسُولٌ قَدْ خَلَتْ مِن قَبْلِهِ ٱلرُّسُلُ أَفَإِيْن مَّاتَ أَوْ قُتِلَ ٱنقَلَبْتُمْ عَلَىٰ أَعْقَٰبِكُمْ وَمَن يَنقَلِبْ عَلَىٰ عَقِبَيْهِ فَلَن يَضُرَّ ٱللَّهَ شَيْئًا وَسَيَجْزِى ٱللَّهُ ٱلشَّٰكِرِينَ (١٤٤)

Muhammad is no more than a Messenger, and indeed (many) Messengers have passed away before him. If he dies or is killed, will you then turn back on your heels (as disbelievers)? And he who turns back on his heels, not the least harm will he do to Allâh, and Allâh will give reward to those who are grateful. (144)

Quran 3:149

يَٰٓأَيُّهَا ٱلَّذِينَ ءَامَنُوٓاْ إِن تُطِيعُواْ ٱلَّذِينَ كَفَرُواْ يَرُدُّوكُمْ عَلَىٰ أَعْقَٰبِكُمْ فَتَنقَلِبُواْ خَٰسِرِينَ (١٤٩)

O you who believe! If you obey those who disbelieve, they will send you back on your heels, and you will turn back (from Faith) as losers. (149)

Quran 3:164

لَقَدْ مَنَّ ٱللَّهُ عَلَى ٱلْمُؤْمِنِينَ إِذْ بَعَثَ فِيهِمْ رَسُولاً مِّنْ أَنفُسِهِمْ يَتْلُواْ عَلَيْهِمْ ءَايَٰتِهِ وَيُزَكِّيهِمْ وَيُعَلِّمُهُمُ ٱلْكِتَٰبَ وَٱلْحِكْمَةَ وَإِن كَانُواْ مِن قَبْلُ لَفِى ضَلَٰلٍ مُّبِينٍ (١٦٤)

Indeed Allâh conferred a great favour on the believers when He sent among them a Messenger (Muhammad) from among themselves, reciting unto them His Verses (the Qur'ân), and purifying them (from sins by their following him), and instructing them (in) the Book (the Qur'ân) and Al¬Hikmah [the wisdom and the Sunnah of the Prophet (i.e. his legal ways, statements, acts of worship)], while before that they had been in manifest error. (164)

Quran 3:196-197

لَا يَغُرَّنَّكَ تَقَلُّبُ ٱلَّذِينَ كَفَرُواْ فِى ٱلْبِلَدِ (١٩٦) مَتَـٰعٌ قَلِيلٌ ثُمَّ مَأْوَىٰهُمْ جَهَنَّمُ وَبِئْسَ ٱلْمِهَادُ (١٩٧)

Let not the free disposal (and affluence) of the disbelievers throughout the land deceive you. (196) A brief enjoyment; then, their ultimate abode is Hell; and worst indeed is that place for rest. (197)

Quran 4:26-27

يُرِيدُ ٱللَّهُ لِيُبَيِّنَ لَكُمْ وَيَهْدِيَكُمْ سُنَنَ ٱلَّذِينَ مِن قَبْلِكُمْ وَيَتُوبَ عَلَيْكُمْ وَٱللَّهُ عَلِيمٌ حَكِيمٌ (٢٦) وَٱللَّهُ يُرِيدُ أَن يَتُوبَ عَلَيْكُمْ وَيُرِيدُ ٱلَّذِينَ يَتَّبِعُونَ ٱلشَّهَوَٰتِ أَن تَمِيلُواْ مَيْلًا عَظِيمًا (٢٧)

Allâh wishes to make clear (what is lawful and what is unlawful) to you, and to show you the ways of those before you, and accept your repentance, and Allâh is All¬Knower, All¬Wise. (26) Allâh wishes to accept your repentance, but those who follow their lusts, wish that you (believers) should deviate tremendously away (from the Right Path). (27)

Quran 4:51-54

أَلَمْ تَرَ إِلَى ٱلَّذِينَ أُوتُواْ نَصِيبًا مِّنَ ٱلْكِتَـٰبِ يُؤْمِنُونَ بِٱلْجِبْتِ وَٱلطَّـٰغُوتِ وَيَقُولُونَ لِلَّذِينَ كَفَرُواْ هَـٰؤُلَاءِ أَهْدَىٰ مِنَ ٱلَّذِينَ ءَامَنُواْ سَبِيلاً (٥١) أُوْلَـٰئِكَ ٱلَّذِينَ لَعَنَهُمُ ٱللَّهُ وَمَن يَلْعَنِ ٱللَّهُ فَلَن تَجِدَ لَهُ نَصِيرًا (٥٢) أَمْ لَهُمْ نَصِيبٌ مِّنَ ٱلْمُلْكِ فَإِذًا لَّا يُؤْتُونَ ٱلنَّاسَ نَقِيرًا (٥٣) أَمْ يَحْسُدُونَ ٱلنَّاسَ عَلَىٰ مَا ءَاتَىٰهُمُ ٱللَّهُ مِن فَضْلِهِ فَقَدْ ءَاتَيْنَا ءَالَ إِبْرَٰهِيمَ ٱلْكِتَـٰبَ وَٱلْحِكْمَةَ وَءَاتَيْنَـٰهُم مُّلْكًا عَظِيمًا (٥٤)

Have you not seen those who were given a portion of the Scripture? They believe in Jibt and Tâghût and say to the disbelievers that they are better guided as regards the way than the believers (Muslims). (51) They are those whom Allâh has cursed, and he whom Allâh curses, you will not find for him (any) helper, (52) Or have they a share in the dominion? Then in that case they would not give mankind even a speck on the back of a date-stone. (53) Or do they envy men (Muhammad and his followers) for what Allâh has given them of His Bounty? Then We had already given the family of Ibrâhim (Abraham) the Book and Al¬Hikmah (As¬Sunnah -

Divine Revelation to those Prophets not written in the form of a book),
and conferred upon them a great kingdom (54)

Quran 4:58-65

﴿ إِنَّ ٱللَّهَ يَأْمُرُكُمْ أَن تُؤَدُّواْ ٱلْأَمَـٰنَـٰتِ إِلَىٰٓ أَهْلِهَا وَإِذَا حَكَمْتُم بَيْنَ ٱلنَّاسِ أَن تَحْكُمُواْ
بِٱلْعَدْلِ ۚ إِنَّ ٱللَّهَ نِعِمَّا يَعِظُكُم بِهِ ۗ إِنَّ ٱللَّهَ كَانَ سَمِيعًا بَصِيرًا (٥٨) يَـٰٓأَيُّهَا ٱلَّذِينَ ءَامَنُوٓاْ
أَطِيعُواْ ٱللَّهَ وَأَطِيعُواْ ٱلرَّسُولَ وَأُوْلِى ٱلْأَمْرِ مِنكُمْ ۖ فَإِن تَنَـٰزَعْتُمْ فِى شَىْءٍ فَرُدُّوهُ إِلَى ٱللَّهِ
وَٱلرَّسُولِ إِن كُنتُمْ تُؤْمِنُونَ بِٱللَّهِ وَٱلْيَوْمِ ٱلْءَاخِرِ ۚ ذَٰلِكَ خَيْرٌ وَأَحْسَنُ تَأْوِيلاً (٥٩) أَلَمْ تَرَ
إِلَى ٱلَّذِينَ يَزْعُمُونَ أَنَّهُمْ ءَامَنُواْ بِمَآ أُنزِلَ إِلَيْكَ وَمَآ أُنزِلَ مِن قَبْلِكَ يُرِيدُونَ أَن
يَتَحَاكَمُوٓاْ إِلَى ٱلطَّـٰغُوتِ وَقَدْ أُمِرُوٓاْ أَن يَكْفُرُواْ بِهِ ۖ وَيُرِيدُ ٱلشَّيْطَـٰنُ أَن يُضِلَّهُمْ ضَلَـٰلاً
بَعِيدًا (٦٠) وَإِذَا قِيلَ لَهُمْ تَعَالَوْاْ إِلَىٰ مَآ أَنزَلَ ٱللَّهُ وَإِلَى ٱلرَّسُولِ رَأَيْتَ ٱلْمُنَـٰفِقِينَ
يَصُدُّونَ عَنكَ صُدُودًا (٦١) فَكَيْفَ إِذَآ أَصَـٰبَتْهُم مُّصِيبَةٌۢ بِمَا قَدَّمَتْ أَيْدِيهِمْ ثُمَّ جَآءُوكَ
يَحْلِفُونَ بِٱللَّهِ إِنْ أَرَدْنَآ إِلَّآ إِحْسَـٰنًا وَتَوْفِيقًا (٦٢) أُوْلَـٰٓئِكَ ٱلَّذِينَ يَعْلَمُ ٱللَّهُ مَا فِى قُلُوبِهِمْ
فَأَعْرِضْ عَنْهُمْ وَعِظْهُمْ وَقُل لَّهُمْ فِىٓ أَنفُسِهِمْ قَوْلاً بَلِيغًا (٦٣) وَمَآ أَرْسَلْنَا مِن رَّسُولٍ
إِلَّا لِيُطَاعَ بِإِذْنِ ٱللَّهِ ۚ وَلَوْ أَنَّهُمْ إِذ ظَّلَمُوٓاْ أَنفُسَهُمْ جَآءُوكَ فَٱسْتَغْفَرُواْ ٱللَّهَ وَٱسْتَغْفَرَ لَهُمُ
ٱلرَّسُولُ لَوَجَدُواْ ٱللَّهَ تَوَّابًا رَّحِيمًا (٦٤) فَلَا وَرَبِّكَ لَا يُؤْمِنُونَ حَتَّىٰ يُحَكِّمُوكَ فِيمَا
شَجَرَ بَيْنَهُمْ ثُمَّ لَا يَجِدُواْ فِىٓ أَنفُسِهِمْ حَرَجًا مِّمَّا قَضَيْتَ وَيُسَلِّمُواْ تَسْلِيمًا (٦٥)

Verily! Allâh commands that you should render back the trusts to those,
to whom they are due; and that when you judge between men, you judge
with justice. Verily, how excellent is the teaching which He (Allâh) gives
you! Truly, Allâh is Ever All¬Hearer, All¬Seer. (58) O you who believe!
Obey Allâh and obey the Messenger (Muhammad), and those of you
(Muslims) who are in authority. (And) if you differ in anything amongst
yourselves, refer it to Allâh and His Messenger, if you believe in Allâh and
in the Last Day. That is better and more suitable for final determination.
(59) Have you seen those (hyprocrites) who claim that they believe in that
which has been sent down to you, and that which was sent down before
you, and they wish to go for judgement (in their disputes) to the Tâghût
(false judges) while they have been ordered to reject them. But Shaitân
(Satan) wishes to lead them far astray. (60) And when it is said to them:
"Come to what Allâh has sent down and to the Messenger (Muhammad),"
you (Muhammad) see the hypocrites turn away from you (Muhammad)
with aversion (61) How then, when a catastrophe befalls them because of

what their hands have sent forth, they come to you swearing by Allâh, "We meant no more than goodwill and conciliation!" (62) They (hypocrites) are those of whom Allâh knows what is in their hearts; so turn aside from them (do not punish them) but admonish them, and speak to them an effective word (i.e. to believe in Allâh, worship Him, obey Him, and be afraid of Him) to reach their innerselves (63) We sent no Messenger, but to be obeyed by Allâh's Leave. If they (hypocrites), when they had been unjust to themselves, had come to you (Muhammad) and begged Allâh's Forgiveness, and the Messenger had begged forgiveness for them: indeed, they would have found Allâh All-Forgiving (One Who forgives and accepts repentance), Most Merciful. (64) But no, by your Lord, they can have no Faith, until they make you (O Muhammad) judge in all disputes between them, and find in themselves no resistance against your decisions, and accept (them) with full submission. (65)

Quran 4:78-85

أَيْنَمَا تَكُونُواْ يُدْرِككُّمُ ٱلْمَوْتُ وَلَوْ كُنتُمْ فِى بُرُوجٍ مُّشَيَّدَةٍ وَإِن تُصِبْهُمْ حَسَنَةٌ يَقُولُواْ هَـٰذِهِۦ مِنْ عِندِ ٱللَّهِ وَإِن تُصِبْهُمْ سَيِّئَةٌ يَقُولُواْ هَـٰذِهِۦ مِنْ عِندِكَ قُلْ كُلٌّ مِّنْ عِندِ ٱللَّهِ فَمَالِ هَـٰٓؤُلَآءِ ٱلْقَوْمِ لَا يَكَادُونَ يَفْقَهُونَ حَدِيثًا (٧٨) مَّآ أَصَابَكَ مِنْ حَسَنَةٍ فَمِنَ ٱللَّهِ وَمَآ أَصَابَكَ مِن سَيِّئَةٍ فَمِن نَّفْسِكَ وَأَرْسَلْنَاكَ لِلنَّاسِ رَسُولًا وَكَفَىٰ بِٱللَّهِ شَهِيدًا (٧٩) مَّن يُطِعِ ٱلرَّسُولَ فَقَدْ أَطَاعَ ٱللَّهَ وَمَن تَوَلَّىٰ فَمَآ أَرْسَلْنَاكَ عَلَيْهِمْ حَفِيظًا (٨٠) وَيَقُولُونَ طَاعَةٌ فَإِذَا بَرَزُواْ مِنْ عِندِكَ بَيَّتَ طَآئِفَةٌ مِّنْهُمْ غَيْرَ ٱلَّذِى تَقُولُ وَٱللَّهُ يَكْتُبُ مَا يُبَيِّتُونَ فَأَعْرِضْ عَنْهُمْ وَتَوَكَّلْ عَلَى ٱللَّهِ وَكَفَىٰ بِٱللَّهِ وَكِيلًا (٨١) أَفَلَا يَتَدَبَّرُونَ ٱلْقُرْءَانَ وَلَوْ كَانَ مِنْ عِندِ غَيْرِ ٱللَّهِ لَوَجَدُواْ فِيهِ ٱخْتِلَٰفًا كَثِيرًا (٨٢) وَإِذَا جَآءَهُمْ أَمْرٌ مِّنَ ٱلْأَمْنِ أَوِ ٱلْخَوْفِ أَذَاعُواْ بِهِۦ وَلَوْ رَدُّوهُ إِلَى ٱلرَّسُولِ وَإِلَىٰٓ أُوْلِى ٱلْأَمْرِ مِنْهُمْ لَعَلِمَهُ ٱلَّذِينَ يَسْتَنۢبِطُونَهُۥ مِنْهُمْ وَلَوْلَا فَضْلُ ٱللَّهِ عَلَيْكُمْ وَرَحْمَتُهُۥ لَٱتَّبَعْتُمُ ٱلشَّيْطَٰنَ إِلَّا قَلِيلًا (٨٣) فَقَٰتِلْ فِى سَبِيلِ ٱللَّهِ لَا تُكَلَّفُ إِلَّا نَفْسَكَ وَحَرِّضِ ٱلْمُؤْمِنِينَ عَسَى ٱللَّهُ أَن يَكُفَّ بَأْسَ ٱلَّذِينَ كَفَرُواْ وَٱللَّهُ أَشَدُّ بَأْسًا وَأَشَدُّ تَنكِيلًا (٨٤) مَّن يَشْفَعْ شَفَٰعَةً حَسَنَةً يَكُن لَّهُۥ نَصِيبٌ مِّنْهَا وَمَن يَشْفَعْ شَفَٰعَةً سَيِّئَةً يَكُن لَّهُۥ كِفْلٌ مِّنْهَا وَكَانَ ٱللَّهُ عَلَىٰ كُلِّ شَىْءٍ مُّقِيتًا (٨٥)

"Wheresoever you may be, death will overtake you even if you are in fortresses built up strong and high!" And if some good reaches them, they say, "This is from Allâh," but if some evil befalls them, they say, "This is from you (O Muhammad)." Say: "All things are from Allâh," so what is wrong with these people that they fail to understand any word? (78) Whatever of good reaches you, is from Allâh, but whatever of evil befalls you, is from yourself. And We have sent you (O Muhammad) as a Messenger to mankind, and Allâh is Sufficient as a Witness. (79) He who obeys the Messenger (Muhammad), has indeed obeyed Allâh, but he who turns away, then we have not sent you (O Muhammad) as a watcher over them. (80) They say: "We are obedient," but when they leave you (Muhammad), a section of them spend all night in planning other than what you say. But Allâh records their nightly (plots). So turn aside from them (do not punish them), and put your trust in Allâh. And Allâh is Ever All¬Sufficient as a Disposer of affairs. (81) Do they not then consider the Qur'ân carefully? Had it been from other than Allâh, they would surely have found therein many contradictions. (82) When there comes to them some matter touching (public) safety or fear, they make it known (among the people), if only they had referred it to the Messenger or to those charged with authority among them, the proper investigators would have understood it from them (directly). Had it not been for the Grace and Mercy of Allâh upon you, you would have followed Shaitân (Satan), save a few of you. (83) Then fight (O Muhammad) in the Cause of Allâh, you are not tasked (held responsible) except for yourself, and incite the believers (to fight along with you), it may be that Allâh will restrain the evil might of the disbelievers. And Allâh is Stronger in Might and Stronger in punishing. (84) Whosoever intercedes for a good cause will have the reward thereof, and whosoever intercedes for an evil cause will have a share in its burden. And Allâh is Ever All-Able to do (and also an All-Witness to) everything. (85)

Quran 4:88-90

۞ فَمَا لَكُمْ فِى ٱلْمُنَٰفِقِينَ فِئَتَيْنِ وَٱللَّهُ أَرْكَسَهُم بِمَا كَسَبُوٓا۟ أَتُرِيدُونَ أَن تَهْدُوا۟ مَنْ أَضَلَّ ٱللَّهُ وَمَن يُضْلِلِ ٱللَّهُ فَلَن تَجِدَ لَهُۥ سَبِيلًا (٨٨) وَدُّوا۟ لَوْ تَكْفُرُونَ كَمَا كَفَرُوا۟ فَتَكُونُونَ سَوَآءٌ فَلَا تَتَّخِذُوا۟ مِنْهُمْ أَوْلِيَآءَ حَتَّىٰ يُهَاجِرُوا۟ فِى سَبِيلِ ٱللَّهِ فَإِن تَوَلَّوْا۟ فَخُذُوهُمْ وَٱقْتُلُوهُمْ حَيْثُ وَجَدتُّمُوهُمْ وَلَا تَتَّخِذُوا۟ مِنْهُمْ وَلِيًّا وَلَا نَصِيرًا (٨٩) إِلَّا ٱلَّذِينَ يَصِلُونَ إِلَىٰ قَوْمٍ بَيْنَكُمْ وَبَيْنَهُم مِّيثَٰقٌ أَوْ جَآءُوكُمْ حَصِرَتْ صُدُورُهُمْ أَن يُقَٰتِلُوكُمْ أَوْ يُقَٰتِلُوا۟ قَوْمَهُمْ وَلَوْ

شَاءَ ٱللَّهُ لَسَلَّطَهُمْ عَلَيْكُمْ فَلَقَٰتَلُوكُمْ فَإِنِ ٱعْتَزَلُوكُمْ فَلَمْ يُقَٰتِلُوكُمْ وَأَلْقَوْاْ إِلَيْكُمُ ٱلسَّلَمَ فَمَا جَعَلَ ٱللَّهُ لَكُمْ عَلَيْهِمْ سَبِيلاً (٩٠)

Then what is the matter with you that you are divided into two parties about the hypocrites? Allâh has cast them back (to disbelief) because of what they have earned. Do you want to guide him whom Allâh has made to go astray? And he whom Allâh has made to go astray, you will never find for him any way (of guidance). (88) They wish that you reject Faith, as they have rejected (Faith), and thus that you all become equal (like one another). So take not Auliyâ' (protectors or friends) from them, till they emigrate in the Way of Allâh. But if they turn back (from Islâm), take (hold of) them and kill them wherever you find them, and take neither Auliyâ' (protectors or friends) nor helpers from them. (89) Except those who join a group, between you and whom there is a treaty (of peace), or those who approach you with their breasts restraining from fighting you as well as fighting their own people. Had Allâh willed, indeed He would have given them power over you, and they would have fought you. So if they withdraw from you, and fight not against you, and offer you peace, then Allâh has opened no way for you against them. (90)

Quran 4:95

لَّا يَسْتَوِى ٱلْقَٰعِدُونَ مِنَ ٱلْمُؤْمِنِينَ غَيْرُ أُوْلِى ٱلضَّرَرِ وَٱلْمُجَٰهِدُونَ فِى سَبِيلِ ٱللَّهِ بِأَمْوَٰلِهِمْ وَأَنفُسِهِمْ فَضَّلَ ٱللَّهُ ٱلْمُجَٰهِدِينَ بِأَمْوَٰلِهِمْ وَأَنفُسِهِمْ عَلَى ٱلْقَٰعِدِينَ دَرَجَةً وَكُلاًّ وَعَدَ ٱللَّهُ ٱلْحُسْنَىٰ وَفَضَّلَ ٱللَّهُ ٱلْمُجَٰهِدِينَ عَلَى ٱلْقَٰعِدِينَ أَجْرًا عَظِيمًا (٩٥)

Not equal are those of the believers who sit (at home), except those who are disabled (by injury or are blind or lame), and those who strive hard and fight in the Cause of Allâh with their wealth and their lives. Allâh has preferred in grades those who strive hard and fight with their wealth and their lives above those who sit (at home). Unto each, Allâh has promised good (Paradise), but Allâh has preferred those who strive hard and fight, above those who sit (at home) by a huge reward; (95)

Quran 4:105

إِنَّا أَنزَلْنَا إِلَيْكَ ٱلْكِتَـٰبَ بِٱلْحَقِّ لِتَحْكُمَ بَيْنَ ٱلنَّاسِ بِمَآ أَرَىٰكَ ٱللَّهُ وَلَا تَكُن لِّلْخَآئِنِينَ خَصِيمًا
(١٠٥)

Surely, We have sent down to you (O Muhammad) the Book (this Qur'ân) in truth that you might judge between men by that which Allâh has shown you (i.e. has taught you through Divine Revelation), so be not a pleader for the treacherous. (105)

Quran 4:115

وَمَن يُشَاقِقِ ٱلرَّسُولَ مِنْ بَعْدِ مَا تَبَيَّنَ لَهُ ٱلْهُدَىٰ وَيَتَّبِعْ غَيْرَ سَبِيلِ ٱلْمُؤْمِنِينَ نُوَلِّهِۦ مَا
تَوَلَّىٰ وَنُصْلِهِۦ جَهَنَّمَ وَسَآءَتْ مَصِيرًا (١١٥)

And whoever contradicts and opposes the Messenger (Muhammad) after the right path has been shown clearly to him, and follows other than the believers' way. We shall keep him in the path he has chosen, and burn him in Hell - what an evil destination. (115)

Quran 4:131-133

وَلِلَّهِ مَا فِى ٱلسَّمَـٰوَٰتِ وَمَا فِى ٱلْأَرْضِ وَلَقَدْ وَصَّيْنَا ٱلَّذِينَ أُوتُواْ ٱلْكِتَـٰبَ مِن قَبْلِكُمْ
وَإِيَّاكُمْ أَنِ ٱتَّقُواْ ٱللَّهَ وَإِن تَكْفُرُواْ فَإِنَّ لِلَّهِ مَا فِى ٱلسَّمَـٰوَٰتِ وَمَا فِى ٱلْأَرْضِ وَكَانَ ٱللَّهُ
غَنِيًّا حَمِيدًا (١٣١) وَلِلَّهِ مَا فِى ٱلسَّمَـٰوَٰتِ وَمَا فِى ٱلْأَرْضِ وَكَفَىٰ بِٱللَّهِ وَكِيلاً
(١٣٢) إِن يَشَأْ يُذْهِبْكُمْ أَيُّهَا ٱلنَّاسُ وَيَأْتِ بِـَٔاخَرِينَ وَكَانَ ٱللَّهُ عَلَىٰ ذَٰلِكَ قَدِيرًا
(١٣٣)

And to Allâh belongs all that is in the heavens and all that is in the earth. And verily, We have recommended to the people of the Scripture before you, and to you (O Muslims) that you (all) fear Allâh, and keep your duty to Him, But if you disbelieve, then unto Allâh belongs all that is in the heavens and all that is in the earth, and Allâh is Ever Rich (Free of all wants), Worthy of all praise. (131) And to Allâh belongs all that is in the heavens and all that is in the earth. And Allâh is Ever All¬Sufficient as a Disposer of affairs. (132) If He wills, He can take you away, O people, and bring others. And Allâh is Ever All¬Potent over that. (133)

Quran 4:135-136

يَٰٓأَيُّهَا ٱلَّذِينَ ءَامَنُوا۟ كُونُوا۟ قَوَّٰمِينَ بِٱلْقِسْطِ شُهَدَآءَ لِلَّهِ وَلَوْ عَلَىٰٓ أَنفُسِكُمْ أَوِ ٱلْوَٰلِدَيْنِ وَٱلْأَقْرَبِينَ إِن يَكُنْ غَنِيًّا أَوْ فَقِيرًا فَٱللَّهُ أَوْلَىٰ بِهِمَا فَلَا تَتَّبِعُوا۟ ٱلْهَوَىٰٓ أَن تَعْدِلُوا۟ وَإِن تَلْوُۥٓا۟ أَوْ تُعْرِضُوا۟ فَإِنَّ ٱللَّهَ كَانَ بِمَا تَعْمَلُونَ خَبِيرًا (١٣٥) يَٰٓأَيُّهَا ٱلَّذِينَ ءَامَنُوٓا۟ ءَامِنُوا۟ بِٱللَّهِ وَرَسُولِهِۦ وَٱلْكِتَٰبِ ٱلَّذِى نَزَّلَ عَلَىٰ رَسُولِهِۦ وَٱلْكِتَٰبِ ٱلَّذِىٓ أَنزَلَ مِن قَبْلُ وَمَن يَكْفُرْ بِٱللَّهِ وَمَلَٰٓئِكَتِهِۦ وَكُتُبِهِۦ وَرُسُلِهِۦ وَٱلْيَوْمِ ٱلْأَخِرِ فَقَدْ ضَلَّ ضَلَٰلًۢا بَعِيدًا (١٣٦)

O you who believe! Stand out firmly for justice, as witnesses to Allâh, even though it be against yourselves, or your parents, or your kin, be he rich or poor, Allâh is a Better Protector to both (than you). So follow not the lusts (of your hearts), lest you avoid justice, and if you distort your witness or refuse to give it, verily, Allâh is Ever Well¬Acquainted with what you do. (135) O you who believe! Believe in Allâh, and His Messenger (Muhammad), and the Book (the Qur'ân) which He has sent down to His Messenger, and the Scripture which He sent down to those before (him), and whosoever disbelieves in Allâh, His Angels, His Books, His Messengers, and the Last Day, then indeed he has strayed far away (136)

Quran 5:12-16

وَلَقَدْ أَخَذَ ٱللَّهُ مِيثَٰقَ بَنِىٓ إِسْرَٰٓءِيلَ وَبَعَثْنَا مِنْهُمُ ٱثْنَىْ عَشَرَ نَقِيبًا وَقَالَ ٱللَّهُ إِنِّى مَعَكُمْ لَئِنْ أَقَمْتُمُ ٱلصَّلَوٰةَ وَءَاتَيْتُمُ ٱلزَّكَوٰةَ وَءَامَنتُم بِرُسُلِى وَعَزَّرْتُمُوهُمْ وَأَقْرَضْتُمُ ٱللَّهَ قَرْضًا حَسَنًا لَّأُكَفِّرَنَّ عَنكُمْ سَيِّـَٔاتِكُمْ وَلَأُدْخِلَنَّكُمْ جَنَّٰتٍ تَجْرِى مِن تَحْتِهَا ٱلْأَنْهَٰرُ فَمَن كَفَرَ بَعْدَ ذَٰلِكَ مِنكُمْ فَقَدْ ضَلَّ سَوَآءَ ٱلسَّبِيلِ (١٢) فَبِمَا نَقْضِهِم مِّيثَٰقَهُمْ لَعَنَّٰهُمْ وَجَعَلْنَا قُلُوبَهُمْ قَٰسِيَةً يُحَرِّفُونَ ٱلْكَلِمَ عَن مَّوَاضِعِهِۦ وَنَسُوا۟ حَظًّا مِّمَّا ذُكِّرُوا۟ بِهِۦ وَلَا تَزَالُ تَطَّلِعُ عَلَىٰ خَآئِنَةٍ مِّنْهُمْ إِلَّا قَلِيلًا مِّنْهُمْ فَٱعْفُ عَنْهُمْ وَٱصْفَحْ إِنَّ ٱللَّهَ يُحِبُّ ٱلْمُحْسِنِينَ (١٣) وَمِنَ ٱلَّذِينَ قَالُوٓا۟ إِنَّا نَصَٰرَىٰٓ أَخَذْنَا مِيثَٰقَهُمْ فَنَسُوا۟ حَظًّا مِّمَّا ذُكِّرُوا۟ بِهِۦ فَأَغْرَيْنَا بَيْنَهُمُ ٱلْعَدَاوَةَ وَٱلْبَغْضَآءَ إِلَىٰ يَوْمِ ٱلْقِيَٰمَةِ وَسَوْفَ يُنَبِّئُهُمُ ٱللَّهُ بِمَا كَانُوا۟ يَصْنَعُونَ (١٤) يَٰٓأَهْلَ ٱلْكِتَٰبِ قَدْ جَآءَكُمْ رَسُولُنَا يُبَيِّنُ لَكُمْ كَثِيرًا مِّمَّا كُنتُمْ تُخْفُونَ مِنَ ٱلْكِتَٰبِ وَيَعْفُوا۟ عَن كَثِيرٍ قَدْ جَآءَكُم مِّنَ ٱللَّهِ نُورٌ وَكِتَٰبٌ مُّبِينٌ (١٥) يَهْدِى بِهِ ٱللَّهُ مَنِ ٱتَّبَعَ رِضْوَٰنَهُۥ سُبُلَ ٱلسَّلَٰمِ وَيُخْرِجُهُم مِّنَ ٱلظُّلُمَٰتِ إِلَى ٱلنُّورِ بِإِذْنِهِۦ وَيَهْدِيهِمْ إِلَىٰ صِرَٰطٍ مُّسْتَقِيمٍ (١٦)

Indeed Allâh took the covenant from the Children of Israel (Jews), and We appointed twelve leaders among them. And Allâh said: "I am with you if you perform As-Salât (Iqâmat-as-Salât) and give Zakât and believe in My Messengers; honour and assist them, and lend a good loan to Allâh. Verily, I will expiate your sins and admit you to Gardens under which rivers flow (in Paradise). But if any of you after this, disbelieved, he has indeed gone astray from the Straight Path." (12) So because of their breach of their covenant, We cursed them, and made their hearts grow hard. They change the words from their (right) places and have abandoned a good part of the Message that was sent to them. And you will not cease to discover deceit in them, except a few of them. But forgive them, and overlook (their misdeeds). Verily, Allâh loves Al¬Muhsinûn (good¬doers). (13) And from those who call themselves Christians, We took their covenant, but they have abandoned a good part of the Message that was sent to them. So We planted amongst them enmity and hatred till the Day of Resurrection (when they discarded Allâh's Book, disobeyed Allâh's Messengers and His Orders and transgressed beyond bounds in Allâh's disobedience), and Allâh will inform them of what they used to do. (14) O people of the Scripture (Jews and Christians)! Now has come to you Our Messenger (Muhammad) explaining to you much of that which you used to hide from the Scripture and pass over (i.e. leaving out without explaining) much. Indeed, there has come to you from Allâh a light and a plain Book (this Qur'ân). (15) Wherewith Allâh guides all those who seek His Good Pleasure to ways of peace, and He brings them out of darkness by His Will unto light and guides them to a Straight Way (Islâmic Monotheism) (16)

Quran 5:19-20

يَٰٓأَهْلَ ٱلْكِتَٰبِ قَدْ جَآءَكُمْ رَسُولُنَا يُبَيِّنُ لَكُمْ عَلَىٰ فَتْرَةٍ مِّنَ ٱلرُّسُلِ أَن تَقُولُوٓاْ مَا جَآءَنَا مِنۢ بَشِيرٍ وَلَا نَذِيرٍ فَقَدْ جَآءَكُم بَشِيرٌ وَنَذِيرٌ وَٱللَّهُ عَلَىٰ كُلِّ شَىْءٍ قَدِيرٌ (١٩) وَإِذْ قَالَ مُوسَىٰ لِقَوْمِهِ يَٰقَوْمِ ٱذْكُرُواْ نِعْمَةَ ٱللَّهِ عَلَيْكُمْ إِذْ جَعَلَ فِيكُمْ أَنۢبِيَآءَ وَجَعَلَكُم مُّلُوكًا وَءَاتَىٰكُم مَّا لَمْ يُؤْتِ أَحَدًا مِّنَ ٱلْعَٰلَمِينَ (٢٠)

O people of the Scripture (Jews and Christians)! Now has come to you Our Messenger (Muhammad) making (things) clear unto you, after a break in (the series of) Messengers, lest you say: "There came unto us no bringer of glad tidings and no warner." But now has come unto you a bringer of glad tidings and a warner. And Allâh is Able to do all things.

(19) And (remember) when Mûsa (Moses) said to his people: "O my people! Remember the Favour of Allâh to you, when He made Prophets among you, made you kings, and gave you what He had not given to any other among the 'Alamîn (mankind and jinn, in the past)." (20)

Quran 5:42-50

سَمَّـٰعُونَ لِلْكَذِبِ أَكَّـٰلُونَ لِلسُّحْتِ فَإِن جَآءُوكَ فَٱحْكُم بَيْنَهُمْ أَوْ أَعْرِضْ عَنْهُمْ وَإِن تُعْرِضْ عَنْهُمْ فَلَن يَضُرُّوكَ شَيْئًا وَإِنْ حَكَمْتَ فَٱحْكُم بَيْنَهُم بِٱلْقِسْطِ إِنَّ ٱللَّهَ يُحِبُّ ٱلْمُقْسِطِينَ (٤٢) وَكَيْفَ يُحَكِّمُونَكَ وَعِندَهُمُ ٱلتَّوْرَىٰةُ فِيهَا حُكْمُ ٱللَّهِ ثُمَّ يَتَوَلَّوْنَ مِنۢ بَعْدِ ذَٰلِكَ وَمَآ أُولَـٰئِكَ بِٱلْمُؤْمِنِينَ (٤٣) إِنَّآ أَنزَلْنَا ٱلتَّوْرَىٰةَ فِيهَا هُدًى وَنُورٌ يَحْكُمُ بِهَا ٱلنَّبِيُّونَ ٱلَّذِينَ أَسْلَمُوا۟ لِلَّذِينَ هَادُوا۟ وَٱلرَّبَّـٰنِيُّونَ وَٱلْأَحْبَارُ بِمَا ٱسْتُحْفِظُوا۟ مِن كِتَـٰبِ ٱللَّهِ وَكَانُوا۟ عَلَيْهِ شُهَدَآءَ فَلَا تَخْشَوُا۟ ٱلنَّاسَ وَٱخْشَوْنِ وَلَا تَشْتَرُوا۟ بِـَٔايَـٰتِى ثَمَنًا قَلِيلًا وَمَن لَّمْ يَحْكُم بِمَآ أَنزَلَ ٱللَّهُ فَأُولَـٰئِكَ هُمُ ٱلْكَـٰفِرُونَ (٤٤) وَكَتَبْنَا عَلَيْهِمْ فِيهَآ أَنَّ ٱلنَّفْسَ بِٱلنَّفْسِ وَٱلْعَيْنَ بِٱلْعَيْنِ وَٱلْأَنفَ بِٱلْأَنفِ وَٱلْأُذُنَ بِٱلْأُذُنِ وَٱلسِّنَّ بِٱلسِّنِّ وَٱلْجُرُوحَ قِصَاصٌ فَمَن تَصَدَّقَ بِهِ فَهُوَ كَفَّارَةٌ لَّهُ وَمَن لَّمْ يَحْكُم بِمَآ أَنزَلَ ٱللَّهُ فَأُولَـٰئِكَ هُمُ ٱلظَّـٰلِمُونَ (٤٥) وَقَفَّيْنَا عَلَىٰٓ ءَاثَـٰرِهِم بِعِيسَى ٱبْنِ مَرْيَمَ مُصَدِّقًا لِّمَا بَيْنَ يَدَيْهِ مِنَ ٱلتَّوْرَىٰةِ وَءَاتَيْنَـٰهُ ٱلْإِنجِيلَ فِيهِ هُدًى وَنُورٌ وَمُصَدِّقًا لِّمَا بَيْنَ يَدَيْهِ مِنَ ٱلتَّوْرَىٰةِ وَهُدًى وَمَوْعِظَةً لِّلْمُتَّقِينَ (٤٦) وَلْيَحْكُمْ أَهْلُ ٱلْإِنجِيلِ بِمَآ أَنزَلَ ٱللَّهُ فِيهِ وَمَن لَّمْ يَحْكُم بِمَآ أَنزَلَ ٱللَّهُ فَأُولَـٰئِكَ هُمُ ٱلْفَـٰسِقُونَ (٤٧) وَأَنزَلْنَآ إِلَيْكَ ٱلْكِتَـٰبَ بِٱلْحَقِّ مُصَدِّقًا لِّمَا بَيْنَ يَدَيْهِ مِنَ ٱلْكِتَـٰبِ وَمُهَيْمِنًا عَلَيْهِ فَٱحْكُم بَيْنَهُم بِمَآ أَنزَلَ ٱللَّهُ وَلَا تَتَّبِعْ أَهْوَآءَهُمْ عَمَّا جَآءَكَ مِنَ ٱلْحَقِّ لِكُلٍّ جَعَلْنَا مِنكُمْ شِرْعَةً وَمِنْهَاجًا وَلَوْ شَآءَ ٱللَّهُ لَجَعَلَكُمْ أُمَّةً وَٰحِدَةً وَلَـٰكِن لِّيَبْلُوَكُمْ فِى مَآ ءَاتَىٰكُمْ فَٱسْتَبِقُوا۟ ٱلْخَيْرَٰتِ إِلَى ٱللَّهِ مَرْجِعُكُمْ جَمِيعًا فَيُنَبِّئُكُم بِمَا كُنتُمْ فِيهِ تَخْتَلِفُونَ (٤٨) وَأَنِ ٱحْكُم بَيْنَهُم بِمَآ أَنزَلَ ٱللَّهُ وَلَا تَتَّبِعْ أَهْوَآءَهُمْ وَٱحْذَرْهُمْ أَن يَفْتِنُوكَ عَنۢ بَعْضِ مَآ أَنزَلَ ٱللَّهُ إِلَيْكَ فَإِن تَوَلَّوْا۟ فَٱعْلَمْ أَنَّمَا يُرِيدُ ٱللَّهُ أَن يُصِيبَهُم بِبَعْضِ ذُنُوبِهِمْ وَإِنَّ كَثِيرًا مِّنَ ٱلنَّاسِ لَفَـٰسِقُونَ (٤٩) أَفَحُكْمَ ٱلْجَـٰهِلِيَّةِ يَبْغُونَ وَمَنْ أَحْسَنُ مِنَ ٱللَّهِ حُكْمًا لِّقَوْمٍ يُوقِنُونَ (٥٠)

(They like to) listen to falsehood, to devour anything forbidden. So if they come to you (O Muhammad), either judge between them, or turn away from them. If you turn away from them, they cannot hurt you in the least. And if you judge, judge with justice between them. Verily, Allâh loves those who act justly. (42) But how do they come to you for decision while they have the Taurât (Torah), in which is the (plain) Decision of Allâh; yet

even after that, they turn away. For they are not (really) believers.
(43) Verily, We did send down the Taurât (Torah) [to Mûsa (Moses)],
therein was guidance and light, by which the Prophets, who submitted
themselves to Allâh's Will, judged for the Jews. And the rabbis and the
priests [too judged for the Jews by the Taurât (Torah) after those Prophets]
for to them was entrusted the protection of Allâh's Book, and they were
witnesses thereto. Therefore fear not men but fear Me (O Jews) and sell
not My Verses for a miserable price. And whosoever does not judge by
what Allâh has revealed, such are the Kâfirûn (i.e. disbelievers - of a lesser
degree as they do not act on Allâh's Laws). (44) And We ordained therein
for them: "Life for life, eye for eye, nose for nose, ear for ear, tooth for
tooth, and wounds equal for equal." But if anyone remits the retaliation by
way of charity, it shall be for him an expiation. And whosoever does not
judge by that which Allâh has revealed, such are the Zâlimûn (polytheists
and wrong¬doers - of a lesser degree). (45) And in their footsteps, We sent
'Īsā (Jesus), son of Maryam (Mary), confirming the Taurât (Torah) that
had come before him, and We gave him the Injeel, in which was guidance
and light and confirmation of the Taurât (Torah) that had come before it, a
guidance and an admonition for Al-Muttaqûn (the pious). (46) Let the
people of the Injeel judge by what Allâh has revealed therein. And
whosoever does not judge by what Allâh has revealed (then) such (people)
are the Fâsiqûn (the rebellious i.e. disobedient (of a lesser degree) to Allâh.
(47) And We have sent down to you (O Muhammad) the Book (this
Qur'ân) in truth, confirming the Scripture that came before it and
Muhaymin (trustworthy in highness and a witness) over it (old
Scriptures). So judge among them by what Allâh has revealed, and follow
not their vain desires, diverging away from the truth that has come to you.
To each among you, We have prescribed a law and a clear way. If Allâh
had willed, He would have made you one nation, but that (He) may test
you in what He has given you; so compete in good deeds. The return of
you (all) is to Allâh; then He will inform you about that in which you used
to differ (48) And so judge among them by what Allâh has revealed and
follow not their vain desires, but beware of them lest they turn you far
away from some of that which Allâh has sent down to you. And if they
turn away, then know that Allâh's Will is to punish them for some sins of

theirs. And truly, most of men are Fâsiqûn (rebellious and disobedient to Allâh). (49) Do they then seek the judgement of (the days of) Ignorance? And who is better in judgement than Allâh for a people who have firm Faith. (50)

Quran 5:65-68

وَلَوْ أَنَّ أَهْلَ ٱلْكِتَـٰبِ ءَامَنُواْ وَٱتَّقَوْاْ لَكَفَّرْنَا عَنْهُمْ سَيِّـَٔاتِهِمْ وَلَأَدْخَلْنَـٰهُمْ جَنَّـٰتِ ٱلنَّعِيمِ (٦٥) وَلَوْ أَنَّهُمْ أَقَامُواْ ٱلتَّوْرَىٰةَ وَٱلْإِنجِيلَ وَمَا أُنزِلَ إِلَيْهِم مِّن رَّبِّهِمْ لَأَكَلُواْ مِن فَوْقِهِمْ وَمِن تَحْتِ أَرْجُلِهِمْ مِّنْهُمْ أُمَّةٌ مُّقْتَصِدَةٌ وَكَثِيرٌ مِّنْهُمْ سَآءَ مَا يَعْمَلُونَ (٦٦) يَـٰٓأَيُّهَا ٱلرَّسُولُ بَلِّغْ مَآ أُنزِلَ إِلَيْكَ مِن رَّبِّكَ وَإِن لَّمْ تَفْعَلْ فَمَا بَلَّغْتَ رِسَالَتَهُ وَٱللَّهُ يَعْصِمُكَ مِنَ ٱلنَّاسِ إِنَّ ٱللَّهَ لَا يَهْدِى ٱلْقَوْمَ ٱلْكَـٰفِرِينَ (٦٧) قُلْ يَـٰٓأَهْلَ ٱلْكِتَـٰبِ لَسْتُمْ عَلَىٰ شَىْءٍ حَتَّىٰ تُقِيمُواْ ٱلتَّوْرَىٰةَ وَٱلْإِنجِيلَ وَمَآ أُنزِلَ إِلَيْكُم مِّن رَّبِّكُمْ وَلَيَزِيدَنَّ كَثِيرًا مِّنْهُم مَّآ أُنزِلَ إِلَيْكَ مِن رَّبِّكَ طُغْيَـٰنًا وَكُفْرًا فَلَا تَأْسَ عَلَى ٱلْقَوْمِ ٱلْكَـٰفِرِينَ (٦٨)

And if only the people of the Scripture (Jews and Christians) had believed (in Muhammad) and warded off evil (sin, ascribing partners to Allâh) and had become Al¬Muttaqûn (the pious) We would indeed have expiated from them their sins and admitted them to Gardens of pleasure (in Paradise). (65) And if only they had acted according to the Taurât (Torah), the Injeel, and what has (now) been sent down to them from their Lord (the Qur'ân), they would surely have gotten provision from above them and from underneath their feet. There are from among them people who are on the right course (i.e. they act on the revelation and believe in Prophet Muhammad), but many of them do evil deeds. (66) O Messenger (Muhamma)! Proclaim (the Message) which has been sent down to you from your Lord. And if you do not, then you have not conveyed His Message. Allâh will protect you from mankind. Verily, Allâh guides not the people who disbelieve. (67) Say "O people of the Scripture (Jews and Christians)! You have nothing (as regards guidance) till you act according to the Taurât (Torah), the Injeel, and what has (now) been sent down to you from your Lord (the Qur'ân)." Verily, that which has been sent down to you (Muhammad) from your Lord increases in most of them (their) obstinate rebellion and disbelief. So be not sorrowful over the people who disbelieve. (68)

Quran 5:104-105

وَإِذَا قِيلَ لَهُمْ تَعَالَوْاْ إِلَىٰ مَآ أَنزَلَ ٱللَّهُ وَإِلَى ٱلرَّسُولِ قَالُواْ حَسْبُنَا مَا وَجَدْنَا عَلَيْهِ ءَابَآءَنَآ أَوَلَوْ كَانَ ءَابَآؤُهُمْ لَا يَعْلَمُونَ شَيْـًٔا وَلَا يَهْتَدُونَ (١٠٤) يَـٰٓأَيُّهَا ٱلَّذِينَ ءَامَنُواْ عَلَيْكُمْ أَنفُسَكُمْ لَا يَضُرُّكُم مَّن ضَلَّ إِذَا ٱهْتَدَيْتُمْ إِلَى ٱللَّهِ مَرْجِعُكُمْ جَمِيعًا فَيُنَبِّئُكُم بِمَا كُنتُمْ تَعْمَلُونَ (١٠٥)

And when it is said to them: "Come to what Allâh has revealed and unto the Messenger (Muhammad for the verdict of that which you have made unlawful)." They say: "Enough for us is that which we found our fathers following," even though their fathers had no knowledge whatsoever and nor guidance. (104) O you who believe! Take care of your ownselves, If you follow the (right) guidance (and enjoin what is right Islâmic Monotheism and all that Islâm orders one to do) and forbid what is wrong (polytheism, disbelief and all that Islâm has forbidden) no hurt can come to you from those who are in error. The return of you all is to Allâh, then He will inform you about (all) that which you used to do. (105)

Quran 6:50

قُل لَّآ أَقُولُ لَكُمْ عِندِى خَزَآئِنُ ٱللَّهِ وَلَآ أَعْلَمُ ٱلْغَيْبَ وَلَآ أَقُولُ لَكُمْ إِنِّى مَلَكٌ إِنْ أَتَّبِعُ إِلَّا مَا يُوحَىٰٓ إِلَىَّ قُلْ هَلْ يَسْتَوِى ٱلْأَعْمَىٰ وَٱلْبَصِيرُ أَفَلَا تَتَفَكَّرُونَ (٥٠)

Say (O Muhammad): "I don't tell you that with me are the treasures of Allâh, nor (that) I know the unseen; nor I tell you that I am an angel. I but follow what is revealed to me." Say: "Are the blind and the one who sees equal? will you not then take thought?" (50)

Quran 6:91

وَمَا قَدَرُواْ ٱللَّهَ حَقَّ قَدْرِهِۦٓ إِذْ قَالُواْ مَآ أَنزَلَ ٱللَّهُ عَلَىٰ بَشَرٍ مِّن شَىْءٍ قُلْ مَنْ أَنزَلَ ٱلْكِتَـٰبَ ٱلَّذِى جَآءَ بِهِۦ مُوسَىٰ نُورًا وَهُدًى لِّلنَّاسِ تَجْعَلُونَهُۥ قَرَاطِيسَ تُبْدُونَهَا وَتُخْفُونَ كَثِيرًا وَعُلِّمْتُم مَّا لَمْ تَعْلَمُوٓاْ أَنتُمْ وَلَآ ءَابَآؤُكُمْ قُلِ ٱللَّهُ ثُمَّ ذَرْهُمْ فِى خَوْضِهِمْ يَلْعَبُونَ (٩١)

They (the Jews, Quraish pagans, idolaters) did not estimate Allâh with an estimation due to Him when they said: "Nothing did Allâh send down to any human being (by revelation)." Say (O Muhammad): "Who then sent down the Book which Mûsa (Moses) brought, a light and a guidance to mankind which you (the Jews) have made into (separate) papersheets, disclosing (some of it) and concealing much. And you (believers in Allâh and His Messenger Muhammad), were taught (through the Qur'ân) that which neither you nor your fathers knew." Say: "Allâh (sent it down)." Then leave them to play in their vain discussions. (91)

Quran 6:114-117

أَفَغَيْرَ ٱللَّهِ أَبْتَغِى حَكَمًا وَهُوَ ٱلَّذِىٓ أَنزَلَ إِلَيْكُمُ ٱلْكِتَٰبَ مُفَصَّلًا وَٱلَّذِينَ ءَاتَيْنَٰهُمُ ٱلْكِتَٰبَ يَعْلَمُونَ أَنَّهُۥ مُنَزَّلٌ مِّن رَّبِّكَ بِٱلْحَقِّ فَلَا تَكُونَنَّ مِنَ ٱلْمُمْتَرِينَ (١١٤) وَتَمَّتْ كَلِمَتُ رَبِّكَ صِدْقًا وَعَدْلًا لَّا مُبَدِّلَ لِكَلِمَٰتِهِۦ وَهُوَ ٱلسَّمِيعُ ٱلْعَلِيمُ (١١٥) وَإِن تُطِعْ أَكْثَرَ مَن فِى ٱلْأَرْضِ يُضِلُّوكَ عَن سَبِيلِ ٱللَّهِ إِن يَتَّبِعُونَ إِلَّا ٱلظَّنَّ وَإِنْ هُمْ إِلَّا يَخْرُصُونَ (١١٦) إِنَّ رَبَّكَ هُوَ أَعْلَمُ مَن يَضِلُّ عَن سَبِيلِهِۦ وَهُوَ أَعْلَمُ بِٱلْمُهْتَدِينَ (١١٧)

[Say (O Muhammad)] "Shall I seek a judge other than Allâh while it is He Who has sent down unto you the Book (the Qur'ân), explained in detail." Those unto whom We gave the Scripture [the Taurât (Torah) and the Injeel] know that it is revealed from your Lord in truth. So be not you of those who doubt. (114) And the Word of your Lord has been fulfilled in truth and in justice. None can change His Words. And He is the All¬Hearer, the All¬Knower. (115) And if you obey most of those on the earth, they will mislead you far away from Allâh's Path. They follow nothing but conjectures, and they do nothing but lie. (116) Verily, your Lord! It is He Who knows best who strays from His Way, and He knows best the rightly guided ones. (117)

Quran 6:122-125

أَوَمَن كَانَ مَيْتًا فَأَحْيَيْنَٰهُ وَجَعَلْنَا لَهُۥ نُورًا يَمْشِى بِهِۦ فِى ٱلنَّاسِ كَمَن مَّثَلُهُۥ فِى ٱلظُّلُمَٰتِ لَيْسَ بِخَارِجٍ مِّنْهَا كَذَٰلِكَ زُيِّنَ لِلْكَٰفِرِينَ مَا كَانُوا۟ يَعْمَلُونَ (١٢٢) وَكَذَٰلِكَ جَعَلْنَا فِى كُلِّ قَرْيَةٍ أَكَٰبِرَ مُجْرِمِيهَا لِيَمْكُرُوا۟ فِيهَا وَمَا يَمْكُرُونَ إِلَّا بِأَنفُسِهِمْ وَمَا يَشْعُرُونَ (١٢٣) وَإِذَا جَآءَتْهُمْ ءَايَةٌ قَالُوا۟ لَن نُّؤْمِنَ حَتَّىٰ نُؤْتَىٰ مِثْلَ مَآ أُوتِىَ رُسُلُ ٱللَّهِ ٱللَّهُ أَعْلَمُ حَيْثُ يَجْعَلُ رِسَالَتَهُۥ سَيُصِيبُ ٱلَّذِينَ أَجْرَمُوا۟ صَغَارٌ عِندَ ٱللَّهِ وَعَذَابٌ شَدِيدٌ بِمَا كَانُوا۟ يَمْكُرُونَ (١٢٤) فَمَن يُرِدِ ٱللَّهُ أَن يَهْدِيَهُۥ يَشْرَحْ صَدْرَهُۥ لِلْإِسْلَٰمِ وَمَن

يُرِدْ أَن يُضِلَّهُ يَجْعَلْ صَدْرَهُ ضَيِّقًا حَرَجًا كَأَنَّمَا يَصَّعَّدُ فِى ٱلسَّمَآءِ كَذَٰلِكَ يَجْعَلُ ٱللَّهُ ٱلرِّجْسَ عَلَى ٱلَّذِينَ لَا يُؤْمِنُونَ (١٢٥)

Is he who was dead (without Faith by ignorance and disbelief) and We gave him life (by knowledge and Faith) and set for him a light (of Belief) whereby he can walk amongst men — like him who is in the darkness (of disbelief, polytheism and hypocrisy) from which he can never come out? Thus it is made fair¬seeming to the disbelievers that which they used to do. (122) And thus We have set up in every town great ones of its wicked people to plot therein. But they plot not except against their ownselves, and they perceive (it) not. (123) And when there comes to them a sign (from Allâh) they say: "We shall not believe until we receive the like of that which the Messengers of Allâh had received." Allâh knows best with whom to place His Message. Humiliation and disgrace from Allâh and a severe torment will overtake the criminals (polytheists, sinners) for that which they used to plot. (124) And whomsoever Allâh wills to guide, He opens his breast to Islâm, and whomsoever He wills to send astray, He makes his breast closed and constricted, as if he is climbing up to the sky. Thus Allâh puts the wrath on those who believe not.(125)

Quran 6:154-157

ثُمَّ ءَاتَيْنَا مُوسَى ٱلْكِتَٰبَ تَمَامًا عَلَى ٱلَّذِىٓ أَحْسَنَ وَتَفْصِيلًا لِّكُلِّ شَىْءٍ وَهُدًى وَرَحْمَةً لَّعَلَّهُم بِلِقَآءِ رَبِّهِمْ يُؤْمِنُونَ (١٥٤) وَهَٰذَا كِتَٰبٌ أَنزَلْنَٰهُ مُبَارَكٌ فَٱتَّبِعُوهُ وَٱتَّقُوا۟ لَعَلَّكُمْ تُرْحَمُونَ (١٥٥) أَن تَقُولُوٓا۟ إِنَّمَآ أُنزِلَ ٱلْكِتَٰبُ عَلَىٰ طَآئِفَتَيْنِ مِن قَبْلِنَا وَإِن كُنَّا عَن دِرَاسَتِهِمْ لَغَٰفِلِينَ (١٥٦) أَوْ تَقُولُوا۟ لَوْ أَنَّآ أُنزِلَ عَلَيْنَا ٱلْكِتَٰبُ لَكُنَّآ أَهْدَىٰ مِنْهُمْ فَقَدْ جَآءَكُم بَيِّنَةٌ مِّن رَّبِّكُمْ وَهُدًى وَرَحْمَةٌ فَمَنْ أَظْلَمُ مِمَّن كَذَّبَ بِـَٔايَٰتِ ٱللَّهِ وَصَدَفَ عَنْهَا سَنَجْزِى ٱلَّذِينَ يَصْدِفُونَ عَنْ ءَايَٰتِنَا سُوٓءَ ٱلْعَذَابِ بِمَا كَانُوا۟ يَصْدِفُونَ (١٥٧)

Then, We gave Mûsa (Moses) the Book [the Taurât (Torah)], to complete (Our Favour) upon those who would do right, and explaining all things in detail and a guidance and a mercy that they might believe in the meeting with their Lord. (154) And this is a blessed Book (the Qur'ân) which We have sent down, so follow it and fear Allâh (i.e. do not disobey His Orders), that you may receive mercy (i.e. be saved from the torment of Hell). (155) Lest you (pagan Arabs) should say: "The Book was sent down only to two sects before us (the Jews and the Christians), and for our part, we were in fact unaware of what they studied." (156) Or lest you (pagan Arabs) should say: "If only the Book had been sent down to us, we would surely have been better guided than they (Jews and Christians)." So now has come unto you a clear proof (the Qur'ân) from your Lord, and a guidance and a mercy. Who then does more wrong than one who rejects the Ayât (proofs, evidences, verses, revelations, etc.) of Allâh and turns away therefrom? We shall requite those who turn away from Our Ayât with an evil torment, because of their turning away (from them). (157)

Quran 6:165

وَهُوَ ٱلَّذِى جَعَلَكُمْ خَلَـٰٓئِفَ ٱلْأَرْضِ وَرَفَعَ بَعْضَكُمْ فَوْقَ بَعْضٍ دَرَجَـٰتٍ لِّيَبْلُوَكُمْ فِى مَآ ءَاتَىٰكُمْ ۗ إِنَّ رَبَّكَ سَرِيعُ ٱلْعِقَابِ وَإِنَّهُۥ لَغَفُورٌ رَّحِيمٌۢ (١٦٥)

And it is He Who has made you generations coming after generations, replacing each other on the earth. And He has raised you in ranks, some above others that He may try you in that which He has bestowed on you. Surely your Lord is Swift in retribution, and certainly He is Oft-Forgiving, Most Merciful. (165)

Quran 7:157-158

ٱلَّذِينَ يَتَّبِعُونَ ٱلرَّسُولَ ٱلنَّبِىَّ ٱلْأُمِّىَّ ٱلَّذِى يَجِدُونَهُۥ مَكْتُوبًا عِندَهُمْ فِى ٱلتَّوْرَىٰةِ وَٱلْإِنجِيلِ يَأْمُرُهُم بِٱلْمَعْرُوفِ وَيَنْهَىٰهُمْ عَنِ ٱلْمُنكَرِ وَيُحِلُّ لَهُمُ ٱلطَّيِّبَـٰتِ وَيُحَرِّمُ عَلَيْهِمُ ٱلْخَبَـٰٓئِثَ وَيَضَعُ عَنْهُمْ إِصْرَهُمْ وَٱلْأَغْلَـٰلَ ٱلَّتِى كَانَتْ عَلَيْهِمْ ۚ فَٱلَّذِينَ ءَامَنُواْ بِهِۦ وَعَزَّرُوهُ وَنَصَرُوهُ وَٱتَّبَعُواْ ٱلنُّورَ ٱلَّذِىٓ أُنزِلَ مَعَهُۥٓ ۙ أُوْلَـٰٓئِكَ هُمُ ٱلْمُفْلِحُونَ (١٥٧) قُلْ يَـٰٓأَيُّهَا ٱلنَّاسُ إِنِّى رَسُولُ ٱللَّهِ إِلَيْكُمْ جَمِيعًا ٱلَّذِى لَهُۥ مُلْكُ ٱلسَّمَـٰوَٰتِ وَٱلْأَرْضِ ۖ لَآ إِلَـٰهَ إِلَّا هُوَ يُحْىِۦ وَيُمِيتُ ۖ فَـَٔامِنُواْ بِٱللَّهِ وَرَسُولِهِ ٱلنَّبِىِّ ٱلْأُمِّىِّ ٱلَّذِى يُؤْمِنُ بِٱللَّهِ وَكَلِمَـٰتِهِۦ وَٱتَّبِعُوهُ لَعَلَّكُمْ تَهْتَدُونَ (١٥٨)

Those who follow the Messenger, the Prophet who can neither read nor write (i.e. Muhammad) whom they find written with them in the Taurât (Torah) and the Injeel, - he commands them for Al-Ma'rûf (i.e. Islâmic Monotheism and all that Islâm has ordained); and forbids them from Al-Munkar (i.e. disbelief, polytheism of all kinds, and all that Islâm has forbidden); he allows them as lawful At-Tayyibât (i.e. all good and lawful as regards things, deeds, beliefs, persons, foods), and prohibits them as unlawful Al-Khabâ'ith (i.e. all evil and unlawful as regards things, deeds, beliefs, persons and foods), he releases them from their heavy burdens (of Allâh's Covenant with the children of Israel), and from the fetters (bindings) that were upon them. So those who believe in him (Muhammad), honour him, help him, and follow the light (the Qur'ân) which has been sent down with him, it is they who will be successful. (157) Say (O Muhammad): "O mankind! Verily, I am sent to you all as the Messenger of Allâh — to Whom belongs the dominion of the heavens and the earth. Lâ ilâha illa Huwa (none has the right to be worshipped but He); It is He Who gives life and causes death. So believe in Allâh and His Messenger (Muhammad), the Prophet who can neither read nor write (i.e. Muhammad) who believes in Allâh and His Words [(this Qur'ân), the Taurât (Torah) and the Injeel and also Allâh's Word: "Be!" - and he was, i.e. 'Īsā (Jesus) son of Maryam (Mary)], and follow him so that you may be guided." (158)

Quran 7:178-179

مَن يَهْدِ ٱللَّهُ فَهُوَ ٱلْمُهْتَدِى ۖ وَمَن يُضْلِلْ فَأُوْلَٰٓئِكَ هُمُ ٱلْخَٰسِرُونَ (١٧٨) وَلَقَدْ ذَرَأْنَا لِجَهَنَّمَ كَثِيرًا مِّنَ ٱلْجِنِّ وَٱلْإِنسِ ۖ لَهُمْ قُلُوبٌ لَّا يَفْقَهُونَ بِهَا وَلَهُمْ أَعْيُنٌ لَّا يُبْصِرُونَ بِهَا وَلَهُمْ ءَاذَانٌ لَّا يَسْمَعُونَ بِهَا ۚ أُوْلَٰٓئِكَ كَٱلْأَنْعَٰمِ بَلْ هُمْ أَضَلُّ ۚ أُوْلَٰٓئِكَ هُمُ ٱلْغَٰفِلُونَ (١٧٩)

Whomsoever Allâh guides, he is the guided one, and whomsoever He sends astray, then those! they are the losers (178) And surely, We have created many of the jinn and mankind for Hell. They have hearts wherewith they understand not, and they have eyes wherewith they see not, and they have ears wherewith they hear not (the truth). They are like cattle, nay even more astray; those! They are the heedless ones. (179)

Quran 7:181-184

وَمِمَّنْ خَلَقْنَآ أُمَّةٌ يَهْدُونَ بِٱلْحَقِّ وَبِهِۦ يَعْدِلُونَ (١٨١) وَٱلَّذِينَ كَذَّبُواْ بِـَٔايَٰتِنَا سَنَسْتَدْرِجُهُم مِّنْ حَيْثُ لَا يَعْلَمُونَ (١٨٢) وَأُمْلِى لَهُمْ ۚ إِنَّ كَيْدِى مَتِينٌ (١٨٣) أَوَلَمْ يَتَفَكَّرُواْ ۗ مَا بِصَاحِبِهِم مِّن جِنَّةٍ ۚ إِنْ هُوَ إِلَّا نَذِيرٌ مُّبِينٌ (١٨٤)

And of those whom We have created, there is a community who guides (others) with the truth, and establishes justice therewith. (181) Those who reject Our Ayât (proofs, evidences, verses, lessons, signs, revelations, etc.), We shall gradually seize them with punishment in ways they perceive not. (182) And I respite them; certainly My Plan is strong. (183) Do they not reflect? There is no madness in their companion (Muhammad). He is but a plain warner. (184)

Quran 8:29

يَـٰٓأَيُّهَا ٱلَّذِينَ ءَامَنُوٓا۟ إِن تَتَّقُوا۟ ٱللَّهَ يَجْعَل لَّكُمْ فُرْقَانًا وَيُكَفِّرْ عَنكُمْ سَيِّـَٔاتِكُمْ وَيَغْفِرْ لَكُمْ وَٱللَّهُ ذُو ٱلْفَضْلِ ٱلْعَظِيمِ (٢٩)

O you who believe! If you obey and fear Allâh, He will grant you Furqân [(a criterion to judge between right and wrong), or (Makhraj, i.e. a way for you to get out from every difficulty)], and will expiate for you your sins, and forgive you; and Allâh is the Owner of the Great Bounty. (29)

Quran 8:73

وَٱلَّذِينَ كَفَرُوا۟ بَعْضُهُمْ أَوْلِيَآءُ بَعْضٍ إِلَّا تَفْعَلُوهُ تَكُن فِتْنَةٌ فِى ٱلْأَرْضِ وَفَسَادٌ كَبِيرٌ (٧٣)

And those who disbelieve are allies of one another, (and) if you (Muslims of the whole world collectively) do not do so [i.e. become allies, as one united block under one Khalifah (a chief Muslim ruler for the whole Muslim world) to make victorious Allâh's religion of Islâmic Monotheism], there will be Fitnah (wars, battles, polytheism) and oppression on the earth, and a great mischief and corruption (appearance of polytheism). (73)

Quran 9:19-20

أَجَعَلْتُمْ سِقَايَةَ ٱلْحَآجِّ وَعِمَارَةَ ٱلْمَسْجِدِ ٱلْحَرَامِ كَمَنْ ءَامَنَ بِٱللَّهِ وَٱلْيَوْمِ ٱلْءَاخِرِ وَجَـٰهَدَ فِى سَبِيلِ ٱللَّهِ لَا يَسْتَوُۥنَ عِندَ ٱللَّهِ وَٱللَّهُ لَا يَهْدِى ٱلْقَوْمَ ٱلظَّـٰلِمِينَ (١٩) ٱلَّذِينَ ءَامَنُوا۟ وَهَاجَرُوا۟ وَجَـٰهَدُوا۟ فِى سَبِيلِ ٱللَّهِ بِأَمْوَٰلِهِمْ وَأَنفُسِهِمْ أَعْظَمُ دَرَجَةً عِندَ ٱللَّهِ وَأُو۟لَـٰٓئِكَ هُمُ ٱلْفَآئِزُونَ (٢٠)

*Do you consider the providing of drinking water to the pilgrims and the
maintenance of Al-Masjid-al-Harâm (at Makkah) as equal to the worth of
those who believe in Allâh and the Last Day, and strive hard and fight in
the Cause of Allâh? They are not equal before Allâh. And Allâh guides not
those people who are the Zâlimûn (polytheists and wrong-doers).
(19) Those who believed (in the Oneness of Allâh - Islâmic Monotheism)
and emigrated and strove hard and fought in Allâh's Cause with their
wealth and their lives are far higher in degree with Allâh. They are the
successful.(20)*

Quran 9:31-33

ٱتَّخَذُوٓاْ أَحْبَارَهُمْ وَرُهْبَـٰنَهُمْ أَرْبَابًا مِّن دُونِ ٱللَّهِ وَٱلْمَسِيحَ ٱبْنَ مَرْيَمَ وَمَآ أُمِرُوٓاْ إِلَّا
لِيَعْبُدُوٓاْ إِلَـٰهًا وَٰحِدًا لَّآ إِلَـٰهَ إِلَّا هُوَ سُبْحَـٰنَهُۥ عَمَّا يُشْرِكُونَ (٣١) يُرِيدُونَ أَن يُطْفِـُٔواْ
نُورَ ٱللَّهِ بِأَفْوَٰهِهِمْ وَيَأْبَى ٱللَّهُ إِلَّآ أَن يُتِمَّ نُورَهُۥ وَلَوْ كَرِهَ ٱلْكَـٰفِرُونَ (٣٢) هُوَ ٱلَّذِىٓ
أَرْسَلَ رَسُولَهُۥ بِٱلْهُدَىٰ وَدِينِ ٱلْحَقِّ لِيُظْهِرَهُۥ عَلَى ٱلدِّينِ كُلِّهِۦ وَلَوْ كَرِهَ ٱلْمُشْرِكُونَ
(٣٣)

*They (Jews and Christians) took their rabbis and their monks to be their
lords besides Allâh (by obeying them in things which they made lawful or
unlawful according to their own desires without being ordered by Allâh),
and (they also took as their Lord) Messiah, son of Maryam (Mary), while
they (Jews and Christians) were commanded [in the Taurât (Torah) and
the Injeel) to worship none but One Ilâh (God - Allâh) Lâ ilâha illa Huwa
(none has the right to be worshipped but He). Praise and glory is to Him,
(far above is He) from having the partners they associate (with Him)."
(31) They (the disbelievers, the Jews and the Christians) want to
extinguish Allâh's Light (with which Muhammad has been sent - Islâmic
Monotheism) with their mouths, but Allâh will not allow except that His
Light should be perfected even though the Kâfirûn (disbelievers) hate (it).
(32) It is He Who has sent His Messenger (Muhammad) with guidance
and the religion of truth (Islâm), to make it superior over all religions even
though the Mushrikûn (polytheists, pagans, idolaters, disbelievers in the
Oneness of Allâh) hate (it). (33)*

Quran 10:35-38

قُلْ هَلْ مِن شُرَكَآئِكُم مَّن يَهْدِىٓ إِلَى ٱلْحَقِّ قُلِ ٱللَّهُ يَهْدِى لِلْحَقِّ أَفَمَن يَهْدِىٓ إِلَى ٱلْحَقِّ
أَحَقُّ أَن يُتَّبَعَ أَمَّن لَّا يَهِدِّىٓ إِلَّآ أَن يُهْدَىٰ فَمَا لَكُمْ كَيْفَ تَحْكُمُونَ (٣٥) وَمَا يَتَّبِعُ
أَكْثَرُهُمْ إِلَّا ظَنًّا إِنَّ ٱلظَّنَّ لَا يُغْنِى مِنَ ٱلْحَقِّ شَيْئًا إِنَّ ٱللَّهَ عَلِيمٌۢ بِمَا يَفْعَلُونَ (٣٦) وَمَا
كَانَ هَٰذَا ٱلْقُرْءَانُ أَن يُفْتَرَىٰ مِن دُونِ ٱللَّهِ وَلَٰكِن تَصْدِيقَ ٱلَّذِى بَيْنَ يَدَيْهِ وَتَفْصِيلَ
ٱلْكِتَٰبِ لَا رَيْبَ فِيهِ مِن رَّبِّ ٱلْعَٰلَمِينَ (٣٧) أَمْ يَقُولُونَ ٱفْتَرَىٰهُ قُلْ فَأْتُوا۟ بِسُورَةٍ مِّثْلِهِۦ
وَٱدْعُوا۟ مَنِ ٱسْتَطَعْتُم مِّن دُونِ ٱللَّهِ إِن كُنتُمْ صَٰدِقِينَ (٣٨)

Say: "Is there of your (Allâh's so-called) partners one that guides to the truth?" Say: "It is Allâh Who guides to the truth. Is then He, Who guides to the truth, more worthy to be followed, or he who finds not guidance (himself) unless he is guided? Then, what is the matter with you? How judge you?" (35) And most of them follow nothing but conjecture. Certainly, conjecture can be of no avail against the truth. Surely, Allâh is All-Aware of what they do. (36) And this Qur'ân is not such as could ever be produced by other than Allâh (Lord of the heavens and the earth), but it is a confirmation of (the revelation) which was before it [i.e. the Taurât (Torah), and the Injeel], and a full explanation of the Book (i.e. laws decreed for mankind) - wherein there is no doubt from the the Lord of the 'Alamîn (mankind, jinn, and all that exists). (37) Or do they say: "He (Muhammad) has forged it?" Say: "Bring then a Sûrah (chapter) like unto it, and call upon whomsoever you can, besides Allâh, if you are truthful!" (38)

Quran 10:108-109

قُلْ يَٰٓأَيُّهَا ٱلنَّاسُ قَدْ جَآءَكُمُ ٱلْحَقُّ مِن رَّبِّكُمْ فَمَنِ ٱهْتَدَىٰ فَإِنَّمَا يَهْتَدِى لِنَفْسِهِۦ وَمَن ضَلَّ
فَإِنَّمَا يَضِلُّ عَلَيْهَا وَمَآ أَنَا۠ عَلَيْكُم بِوَكِيلٍ (١٠٨) وَٱتَّبِعْ مَا يُوحَىٰٓ إِلَيْكَ وَٱصْبِرْ حَتَّىٰ
يَحْكُمَ ٱللَّهُ وَهُوَ خَيْرُ ٱلْحَٰكِمِينَ (١٠٩)

Say: "O you mankind! Now truth (i.e. the Qur'ân and Prophet Muhammad), has come to you from your Lord. So whosoever receives guidance, he does so for the good of his own self, and whosoever goes astray, he does so to his own loss, and I am not (set) over you as a Wakîl (disposer of affairs to oblige you for guidance)." (108) And (O Muhammad), follow the revelation sent unto you, and be patient till Allâh gives judgement. And He is the Best of judges. (109)

Quran 11:17

أَفَمَن كَانَ عَلَىٰ بَيِّنَةٍ مِّن رَّبِّهِ وَيَتْلُوهُ شَاهِدٌ مِّنْهُ وَمِن قَبْلِهِ كِتَابُ مُوسَىٰ إِمَامًا وَرَحْمَةً أُوْلَٰئِكَ يُؤْمِنُونَ بِهِ وَمَن يَكْفُرْ بِهِ مِنَ ٱلْأَحْزَابِ فَٱلنَّارُ مَوْعِدُهُ فَلَا تَكُ فِى مِرْيَةٍ مِّنْهُ إِنَّهُ ٱلْحَقُّ مِن رَّبِّكَ وَلَٰكِنَّ أَكْثَرَ ٱلنَّاسِ لَا يُؤْمِنُونَ (١٧)

Can they (Muslims) who rely on a clear proof (the Qur'ân) from their Lord, and whom a witness [Jibrail (Gabriel] from Him recites (follows) it (can they be equal with the disbelievers); and before it, came the Book of Mûsa (Moses), a guidance and a mercy, they believe therein, but those of the sects (Jews, Christians and all the other non-Muslim nations) that reject it (the Qur'ân), the Fire will be their promised meeting-place. So be not in doubt about it (i.e. those who denied Prophet Muhammad and also denied all that which he brought from Allâh, surely, they will enter Hell). Verily, it is the truth from your Lord, but most of mankind believe not (17)

Quran 11:24

۞ مَثَلُ ٱلْفَرِيقَيْنِ كَٱلْأَعْمَىٰ وَٱلْأَصَمِّ وَٱلْبَصِيرِ وَٱلسَّمِيعِ هَلْ يَسْتَوِيَانِ مَثَلًا أَفَلَا تَذَكَّرُونَ (٢٤)

The likeness of the two parties is as the blind and the deaf and the seer and the hearer. Are they equal when compared? Will you not then take heed? (24)

Quran 12:38

وَٱتَّبَعْتُ مِلَّةَ ءَابَآءِى إِبْرَاهِيمَ وَإِسْحَاقَ وَيَعْقُوبَ مَا كَانَ لَنَا أَن نُّشْرِكَ بِٱللَّهِ مِن شَىْءٍ ذَٰلِكَ مِن فَضْلِ ٱللَّهِ عَلَيْنَا وَعَلَى ٱلنَّاسِ وَلَٰكِنَّ أَكْثَرَ ٱلنَّاسِ لَا يَشْكُرُونَ (٣٨)

"And I have followed the religion of my fathers, - Ibrâhîm (Abraham), Ishâq (Isaac) and Ya'qûb (Jacob), and never could we attribute any partners whatsoever to Allâh. This is from the Grace of Allâh to us and to mankind, but most men thank not (i.e. they neither believe in Allâh, nor worship Him). (38)

Quran 12:111

لَقَدْ كَانَ فِى قَصَصِهِمْ عِبْرَةٌ لِّأُوْلِى ٱلْأَلْبَٰبِ مَا كَانَ حَدِيثًا يُفْتَرَىٰ وَلَٰكِن تَصْدِيقَ ٱلَّذِى بَيْنَ يَدَيْهِ وَتَفْصِيلَ كُلِّ شَىْءٍ وَهُدًى وَرَحْمَةً لِّقَوْمٍ يُؤْمِنُونَ (١١١)

Indeed in their stories, there is a lesson for men of understanding. It (the Quran) is not a forged statement but a confirmation of Allâhs existing Books which were before it [the Taurât (Torah), the Injeel and other Scriptures of Allâh] and a detailed explanation of everything and a guide and a Mercy for the people who believe. (111)

Quran 13:37

وَكَذَٰلِكَ أَنزَلْنَٰهُ حُكْمًا عَرَبِيًّا وَلَئِنِ ٱتَّبَعْتَ أَهْوَآءَهُم بَعْدَمَا جَآءَكَ مِنَ ٱلْعِلْمِ مَا لَكَ مِنَ ٱللَّهِ مِن وَلِيٍّ وَلَا وَاقٍ (٣٧)

And thus have We sent it (the Qur'ân) down to be a judgement of authority in Arabic. Were you (O Muhammad) to follow their (vain) desires after the knowledge which has come to you, then you will not have any Walî (protector) or Waq (defender) against Allâh. (37)

Quran 16:75-76

۞ ضَرَبَ ٱللَّهُ مَثَلًا عَبْدًا مَّمْلُوكًا لَّا يَقْدِرُ عَلَىٰ شَىْءٍ وَمَن رَّزَقْنَٰهُ مِنَّا رِزْقًا حَسَنًا فَهُوَ يُنفِقُ مِنْهُ سِرًّا وَجَهْرًا هَلْ يَسْتَوُۥنَ ٱلْحَمْدُ لِلَّهِ بَلْ أَكْثَرُهُمْ لَا يَعْلَمُونَ (٧٥) وَضَرَبَ ٱللَّهُ مَثَلًا رَّجُلَيْنِ أَحَدُهُمَا أَبْكَمُ لَا يَقْدِرُ عَلَىٰ شَىْءٍ وَهُوَ كَلٌّ عَلَىٰ مَوْلَىٰهُ أَيْنَمَا يُوَجِّههُّ لَا يَأْتِ بِخَيْرٍ هَلْ يَسْتَوِى هُوَ وَمَن يَأْمُرُ بِٱلْعَدْلِ وَهُوَ عَلَىٰ صِرَٰطٍ مُّسْتَقِيمٍ (٧٦)

Allâh puts forward the example (of two men — a believer and a disbeliever); a slave (disbeliever) under the possession of another, he has no power of any sort, and (the other), a man (believer) on whom We have bestowed a good provision from Us, and he spends thereof secretly and openly. Can they be equal? (By no means). All the praises and thanks are to Allâh. Nay! (But) most of them know not. (75) And Allâh puts forward (another) example of two men, one of them dumb, who has no power over anything (disbeliever), and he is a burden on his master, whichever way he directs him, he brings no good. Is such a man equal to one (believer in the

Islâmic Monotheism) who commands justice, and is himself on a Straight
Path? (76)

Quran 16:89

وَيَوْمَ نَبْعَثُ فِى كُلِّ أُمَّةٍ شَهِيدًا عَلَيْهِم مِّنْ أَنفُسِهِمْ وَجِئْنَا بِكَ شَهِيدًا عَلَىٰ هَـٰٓؤُلَآءِ وَنَزَّلْنَا
عَلَيْكَ ٱلْكِتَـٰبَ تِبْيَـٰنًا لِّكُلِّ شَىْءٍ وَهُدًى وَرَحْمَةً وَبُشْرَىٰ لِلْمُسْلِمِينَ (٨٩)

And (remember) the Day when We shall raise up from every nation a
witness against them from amongst themselves. And We shall bring you
(O Muhammad) as a witness against these. And We have sent down to
you the Book (the Qur'an) as an exposition of everything, a guidance, a
mercy, and glad tidings for those who have submitted themselves (to Allâh
as Muslims). (89)

Quran 16:93-95

وَلَوْ شَآءَ ٱللَّهُ لَجَعَلَكُمْ أُمَّةً وَٰحِدَةً وَلَـٰكِن يُضِلُّ مَن يَشَآءُ وَيَهْدِى مَن يَشَآءُ وَلَتُسْـَٔلُنَّ
عَمَّا كُنتُمْ تَعْمَلُونَ (٩٣) وَلَا تَتَّخِذُوٓاْ أَيْمَـٰنَكُمْ دَخَلًۢا بَيْنَكُمْ فَتَزِلَّ قَدَمٌۢ بَعْدَ ثُبُوتِهَا
وَتَذُوقُواْ ٱلسُّوٓءَ بِمَا صَدَدتُّمْ عَن سَبِيلِ ٱللَّهِ وَلَكُمْ عَذَابٌ عَظِيمٌ (٩٤) وَلَا تَشْتَرُواْ بِعَهْدِ
ٱللَّهِ ثَمَنًا قَلِيلًا إِنَّمَا عِندَ ٱللَّهِ هُوَ خَيْرٌ لَّكُمْ إِن كُنتُمْ تَعْلَمُونَ (٩٥)

And had Allâh willed, He could have made you (all) one nation, but He
sends astray whom He wills and guides whom He wills. But you shall
certainly be called to account for what you used to do. (93) And make not
your oaths, a means of deception among yourselves, lest a foot should slip
after being firmly planted, and you may have to taste the evil (punishment
in this world) of having hindered (men) from the Path of Allâh (i.e. Belief
in the Oneness of Allâh and His Messenger, Muhammad), and yours will
be a great torment (i.e. the Fire of Hell in the Hereafter). (94) And
purchase not a small gain at the cost of Allâh's Covenant. Verily! What is
with Allâh is better for you if you did but know. (95)

Quran 17:2

وَءَاتَيْنَا مُوسَى ٱلْكِتَـٰبَ وَجَعَلْنَـٰهُ هُدًى لِّبَنِىٓ إِسْرَٰٓءِيلَ أَلَّا تَتَّخِذُواْ مِن دُونِى وَكِيلًا (٢)

And We gave Mûsa (Moses) the Scripture and made it a guidance for the Children of Israel (saying): "Take not other than Me as (your) Wakîl (Protector, Lord, or Disposer of your affairs). (2)

Quran 17:9

إِنَّ هَـٰذَا ٱلْقُرْءَانَ يَهْدِى لِلَّتِى هِىَ أَقْوَمُ وَيُبَشِّرُ ٱلْمُؤْمِنِينَ ٱلَّذِينَ يَعْمَلُونَ ٱلصَّـٰلِحَـٰتِ أَنَّ لَهُمْ أَجْرًا كَبِيرًا (٩)

Verily, this Qur'ân guides to that which is most just and right and gives glad tidings to the believers (in the Oneness of Allâh and His Messenger, Muhammad). who work deeds of righteousness, that they shall have a great reward (Paradise). (9)

Quran 17:39

ذَٰلِكَ مِمَّا أَوْحَىٰ إِلَيْكَ رَبُّكَ مِنَ ٱلْحِكْمَةِ وَلَا تَجْعَلْ مَعَ ٱللَّهِ إِلَـٰهًا ءَاخَرَ فَتُلْقَىٰ فِى جَهَنَّمَ مَلُومًا مَّدْحُورًا (٣٩)

This is (part) of Al-Hikmah (wisdom, good manners and high character) which your Lord has revealed to you (O Muhammad). And set not up with Allâh any other ilâh (god) lest you should be thrown into Hell, blameworthy and rejected, (from Allâh's Mercy). (39)

Quran 17:41

وَلَقَدْ صَرَّفْنَا فِى هَـٰذَا ٱلْقُرْءَانِ لِيَذَّكَّرُوا وَمَا يَزِيدُهُمْ إِلَّا نُفُورًا (٤١)

And surely, We have explained [Our Promises, Warnings and (set forth many) examples] in this Qur'ân that they (the disbelievers) may take heed, but it increases them in naught save aversion. (41)

Quran 17:73-77

وَإِن كَادُوا لَيَفْتِنُونَكَ عَنِ ٱلَّذِى أَوْحَيْنَا إِلَيْكَ لِتَفْتَرِىَ عَلَيْنَا غَيْرَهُ وَإِذًا لَّٱتَّخَذُوكَ خَلِيلًا (٧٣) وَلَوْلَا أَن ثَبَّتْنَاكَ لَقَدْ كِدتَّ تَرْكَنُ إِلَيْهِمْ شَيْئًا قَلِيلًا (٧٤) إِذًا لَّأَذَقْنَاكَ ضِعْفَ ٱلْحَيَوٰةِ وَضِعْفَ ٱلْمَمَاتِ ثُمَّ لَا تَجِدُ لَكَ عَلَيْنَا نَصِيرًا (٧٥) وَإِن كَادُوا لَيَسْتَفِزُّونَكَ مِنَ ٱلْأَرْضِ لِيُخْرِجُوكَ مِنْهَا وَإِذًا لَّا يَلْبَثُونَ خِلَٰفَكَ إِلَّا قَلِيلًا (٧٦) سُنَّةَ مَن قَدْ أَرْسَلْنَا قَبْلَكَ مِن رُّسُلِنَا وَلَا تَجِدُ لِسُنَّتِنَا تَحْوِيلًا (٧٧)

Verily, they were about to tempt you away from that which We have revealed (the Qur'ân) unto you (O Muhammad), to fabricate something other than it against Us, and then they would certainly have taken you a Khalil (an intimate friend)! (73) And had We not made you stand firm, you would nearly have inclined to them a little. (74) In that case, We would have made you taste a double portion (of punishment) in this life and a double portion (of punishment) after death. And then you would have found none to help you against Us. (75) And Verily, they were about to frighten you so much as to drive you out from the land. But in that case they would not have stayed (therein) after you, except for a little while. (76) (This was Our) Sunnah (rule or way) with the Messengers We sent before you (O Muhammad), and you will not find any alteration in Our Sunnah (rule or way). (77)

Quran 24:48-51

وَإِذَا دُعُوٓاْ إِلَى ٱللَّهِ وَرَسُولِهِۦ لِيَحْكُمَ بَيْنَهُمْ إِذَا فَرِيقٌ مِّنْهُم مُّعْرِضُونَ (٤٨) وَإِن يَكُن لَّهُمُ ٱلْحَقُّ يَأْتُوٓاْ إِلَيْهِ مُذْعِنِينَ (٤٩) أَفِى قُلُوبِهِم مَّرَضٌ أَمِ ٱرْتَابُوٓاْ أَمْ يَخَافُونَ أَن يَحِيفَ ٱللَّهُ عَلَيْهِمْ وَرَسُولُهُۥ بَلْ أُوْلَٰٓئِكَ هُمُ ٱلظَّٰلِمُونَ (٥٠) إِنَّمَا كَانَ قَوْلَ ٱلْمُؤْمِنِينَ إِذَا دُعُوٓاْ إِلَى ٱللَّهِ وَرَسُولِهِۦ لِيَحْكُمَ بَيْنَهُمْ أَن يَقُولُواْ سَمِعْنَا وَأَطَعْنَا وَأُوْلَٰٓئِكَ هُمُ ٱلْمُفْلِحُونَ (٥١)

And when they are called to Allâh (i.e. His Words, the Qur'ân) and His Messenger, to judge between them, lo! a party of them refuse (to come) and turn away. (48) But if the truth is on their sides, they come to him willingly with submission. (49) Is there a disease in their hearts? Or do they doubt or fear lest Allâh and His Messenger should wrong them in judgement. Nay, it is they themselves who are the Zâlimûn (polytheists, hypocrites and wrong-doers). (50) The only saying of the faithful believers, when they are called to Allâh (His Words, the Qur'ân) and His Messenger, to judge between them, is that they say: "We hear and we obey." And such are the successful (who will live forever in Paradise). (51)

Quran 24:55

وَعَدَ ٱللَّهُ ٱلَّذِينَ ءَامَنُواْ مِنكُمْ وَعَمِلُواْ ٱلصَّـٰلِحَـٰتِ لَيَسْتَخْلِفَنَّهُمْ فِى ٱلْأَرْضِ كَمَا ٱسْتَخْلَفَ ٱلَّذِينَ مِن قَبْلِهِمْ وَلَيُمَكِّنَنَّ لَهُمْ دِينَهُمُ ٱلَّذِى ٱرْتَضَىٰ لَهُمْ وَلَيُبَدِّلَنَّهُم مِّنۢ بَعْدِ خَوْفِهِمْ أَمْنًا يَعْبُدُونَنِى لَا يُشْرِكُونَ بِى شَيْـًٔا وَمَن كَفَرَ بَعْدَ ذَٰلِكَ فَأُوْلَـٰٓئِكَ هُمُ ٱلْفَـٰسِقُونَ (٥٥)

Allâh has promised those among you who believe, and do righteous good deeds, that He will certainly grant them succession to (the present rulers) in the land, as He granted it to those before them, and that He will grant them the authority to practice their religion, which He has chosen for them (i.e. Islâm). And He will surely give them in exchange a safe security after their fear (provided) they (believers) worship Me and do not associate anything (in worship) with Me. But whoever disbelieves after this, they are the Fâsiqûn (rebellious, disobedient to Allâh). (55)

Quran 25:1

تَبَارَكَ ٱلَّذِى نَزَّلَ ٱلْفُرْقَانَ عَلَىٰ عَبْدِهِۦ لِيَكُونَ لِلْعَـٰلَمِينَ نَذِيرًا (١)

Blessed is He Who sent down the criterion (of right and wrong, i.e. this Qur'ân) to His slave (Muhammad) that he may be a warner to the 'Alamîn (mankind and jinn). (1)

Quran 25:30

وَقَالَ ٱلرَّسُولُ يَـٰرَبِّ إِنَّ قَوْمِى ٱتَّخَذُواْ هَـٰذَا ٱلْقُرْءَانَ مَهْجُورًا (٣٠)

And the Messenger (Muhammad) will say: "O my Lord! Verily, my people deserted this Qur'ân (neither listened to it, nor acted on its laws and teachings). (30)

Quran 27:15

وَلَقَدْ ءَاتَيْنَا دَاوُۥدَ وَسُلَيْمَـٰنَ عِلْمًا وَقَالَا ٱلْحَمْدُ لِلَّهِ ٱلَّذِى فَضَّلَنَا عَلَىٰ كَثِيرٍ مِّنْ عِبَادِهِ ٱلْمُؤْمِنِينَ (١٥)

And indeed We gave knowledge to Dawûd (David) and Sulaimân (Solomon), and they both said: "All the praises and thanks are to Allâh, Who has preferred us above many of His believing slaves!" (15)

Quran 28:43

وَلَقَدْ ءَاتَيْنَا مُوسَى ٱلْكِتَـٰبَ مِنۢ بَعْدِ مَآ أَهْلَكْنَا ٱلْقُرُونَ ٱلْأُولَىٰ بَصَآئِرَ لِلنَّاسِ وَهُدًى وَرَحْمَةً لَّعَلَّهُمْ يَتَذَكَّرُونَ (٤٣)

And indeed We gave Mûsa (Moses), after We had destroyed the generations of old, — the Scripture [the Taurât (Torah)] as an enlightenment for mankind, and a guidance and a mercy, that they might remember (or receive admonition). (43)

Quran 28:48-52

فَلَمَّا جَآءَهُمُ ٱلْحَقُّ مِنْ عِندِنَا قَالُوا۟ لَوْلَا أُوتِىَ مِثْلَ مَآ أُوتِىَ مُوسَىٰٓ أَوَلَمْ يَكْفُرُوا۟ بِمَآ أُوتِىَ مُوسَىٰ مِن قَبْلُ قَالُوا۟ سِحْرَانِ تَظَـٰهَرَا وَقَالُوٓا۟ إِنَّا بِكُلٍّ كَـٰفِرُونَ (٤٨) قُلْ فَأْتُوا۟ بِكِتَـٰبٍ مِّنْ عِندِ ٱللَّهِ هُوَ أَهْدَىٰ مِنْهُمَآ أَتَّبِعْهُ إِن كُنتُمْ صَـٰدِقِينَ (٤٩) فَإِن لَّمْ يَسْتَجِيبُوا۟ لَكَ فَٱعْلَمْ أَنَّمَا يَتَّبِعُونَ أَهْوَآءَهُمْ وَمَنْ أَضَلُّ مِمَّنِ ٱتَّبَعَ هَوَىٰهُ بِغَيْرِ هُدًى مِّنَ ٱللَّهِ إِنَّ ٱللَّهَ لَا يَهْدِى ٱلْقَوْمَ ٱلظَّـٰلِمِينَ (٥٠) ۞ وَلَقَدْ وَصَّلْنَا لَهُمُ ٱلْقَوْلَ لَعَلَّهُمْ يَتَذَكَّرُونَ (٥١) ٱلَّذِينَ ءَاتَيْنَـٰهُمُ ٱلْكِتَـٰبَ مِن قَبْلِهِۦ هُم بِهِۦ يُؤْمِنُونَ (٥٢)

But when the truth (i.e. Muhammad with his Message) has come to them from Us, they say: "Why is he not given the like of what was given to Mûsa (Moses)? Did they not disbelieve in that which was given to Mûsa (Moses) of old? They say: "Two kinds of magic [the Taurât (Torah) and the Qur'ân] each helping the other!" And they say: "Verily! In both we are disbelievers." (48) Say (to them, O Muhammad): "Then bring a Book from Allâh, which is a better guide than these two [the Taurât (Torah) and the Qur'ân], that I may follow it, if you are truthful." (49) But if they answer you not (i.e. do not bring the book nor believe in your doctrine of Islâmic Monotheism), then know that they only follow their own lusts. And who is more astray than one who follows his own lusts, without guidance from Allâh? Verily! Allâh guides not the people who are Zâlimûn (wrong-doers, disobedient to Allâh, and polytheists) (50) And indeed now We have conveyed the Word (this Qur'ân in which is the news of everything) to them, in order that they may remember (or receive admonition). (51) Those to whom We gave the Scripture [i.e. the Taurât (Torah) and the Injeel] before it, - they believe in it (the Qur'ân). (52)

Quran 28:75

وَنَزَعْنَا مِن كُلِّ أُمَّةٍ شَهِيدًا فَقُلْنَا هَاتُوا بُرْهَٰنَكُمْ فَعَلِمُوا أَنَّ ٱلْحَقَّ لِلَّهِ وَضَلَّ عَنْهُم مَّا كَانُوا يَفْتَرُونَ (٧٥)

And We shall take out from every nation a witness, and We shall say: "Bring your proof." Then they shall know that the truth is with Allâh (Alone), and the lies (false gods) which they invented will disappear from them. (75)

Quran 28:85-86

إِنَّ ٱلَّذِى فَرَضَ عَلَيْكَ ٱلْقُرْءَانَ لَرَآدُّكَ إِلَىٰ مَعَادٍ ۚ قُل رَّبِّى أَعْلَمُ مَن جَآءَ بِٱلْهُدَىٰ وَمَنْ هُوَ فِى ضَلَٰلٍ مُّبِينٍ (٨٥) وَمَا كُنتَ تَرْجُوا أَن يُلْقَىٰ إِلَيْكَ ٱلْكِتَٰبُ إِلَّا رَحْمَةً مِّن رَّبِّكَ فَلَا تَكُونَنَّ ظَهِيرًا لِّلْكَٰفِرِينَ (٨٦)

Verily, He Who has given you (O Muhammad) the Qur'an (i.e. ordered you to act on its laws and to preach it to others) will surely bring you back to the Ma'âd (place of return, either to Makkah or to Paradise after your death, etc.). Say (O Muhammad): "My Lord is Aware of him who brings guidance, and of him who is in manifest error." (85) And you were not expecting that the Book (this Qur'ân) would be sent down to you, but it is a mercy from your Lord. So never be a supporter of the disbelievers. (86)

Quran 33:36

وَمَا كَانَ لِمُؤْمِنٍ وَلَا مُؤْمِنَةٍ إِذَا قَضَى ٱللَّهُ وَرَسُولُهُ أَمْرًا أَن يَكُونَ لَهُمُ ٱلْخِيَرَةُ مِنْ أَمْرِهِمْ ۗ وَمَن يَعْصِ ٱللَّهَ وَرَسُولَهُ فَقَدْ ضَلَّ ضَلَٰلًا مُّبِينًا (٣٦)

It is not for a believer, man or woman, when Allâh and His Messenger have decreed a matter that they should have any option in their decision. And whoever disobeys Allâh and His Messenger, he has indeed strayed in to a plain error. (36)

Quran 36:2-7

وَٱلْقُرْءَانِ ٱلْحَكِيمِ (٢) إِنَّكَ لَمِنَ ٱلْمُرْسَلِينَ (٣) عَلَىٰ صِرَٰطٍ مُّسْتَقِيمٍ (٤) تَنزِيلَ ٱلْعَزِيزِ ٱلرَّحِيمِ (٥) لِتُنذِرَ قَوْمًا مَّآ أُنذِرَ ءَابَآؤُهُمْ فَهُمْ غَٰفِلُونَ (٦) لَقَدْ حَقَّ ٱلْقَوْلُ عَلَىٰ أَكْثَرِهِمْ فَهُمْ لَا يُؤْمِنُونَ (٧)

By the Qur'ân, full of wisdom (i.e. full of laws, evidences, and proofs), (2) Truly, you (O Muhammad) are one of the Messengers, (3) On the Straight Path (i.e. on Allâh's religion of Islâmic Monotheism). (4) (This is a Revelation) sent down by the All¬Mighty, the Most Merciful, (5) In order that you may warn a people whose forefathers were not warned, so they are heedless. (6) Indeed the Word (of punishment) has proved true against most of them, so they will not believe. (7)

Quran 37:69-74

إِنَّهُمْ أَلْفَوْا۟ ءَابَآءَهُمْ ضَآلِّينَ (٦٩) فَهُمْ عَلَىٰ ءَاثَٰرِهِمْ يُهْرَعُونَ (٧٠) وَلَقَدْ ضَلَّ قَبْلَهُمْ أَكْثَرُ ٱلْأَوَّلِينَ (٧١) وَلَقَدْ أَرْسَلْنَا فِيهِم مُّنذِرِينَ (٧٢) فَٱنظُرْ كَيْفَ كَانَ عَٰقِبَةُ ٱلْمُنذَرِينَ (٧٣) إِلَّا عِبَادَ ٱللَّهِ ٱلْمُخْلَصِينَ (٧٤)

Verily, they found their fathers on the wrong path; (69) So they (too) hastened in their footsteps! (70) And indeed most of the men of old went astray before them; (71) And indeed We sent among them warners (Messengers); (72) Then see what was the end of those who were warned (but heeded not). (73) Except the chosen slaves of Allâh (faithful, obedient, and true believers of Islâmic Monotheism). (74)

Quran 38:26

يَٰدَاوُۥدُ إِنَّا جَعَلْنَٰكَ خَلِيفَةً فِى ٱلْأَرْضِ فَٱحْكُم بَيْنَ ٱلنَّاسِ بِٱلْحَقِّ وَلَا تَتَّبِعِ ٱلْهَوَىٰ فَيُضِلَّكَ عَن سَبِيلِ ٱللَّهِ إِنَّ ٱلَّذِينَ يَضِلُّونَ عَن سَبِيلِ ٱللَّهِ لَهُمْ عَذَابٌ شَدِيدٌۢ بِمَا نَسُوا۟ يَوْمَ ٱلْحِسَابِ (٢٦)

O Dâwûd (David)! Verily! We have placed you as a successor on earth, so judge you between men in truth (and justice) and follow not your desire for it will mislead you from the Path of Allâh. Verily! those who wander astray from the Path of Allâh (shall) have a severe torment, because they forgot the Day of Reckoning. (26)

Quran 38:28-29

أَمْ نَجْعَلُ ٱلَّذِينَ ءَامَنُواْ وَعَمِلُواْ ٱلصَّٰلِحَٰتِ كَٱلْمُفْسِدِينَ فِى ٱلْأَرْضِ أَمْ نَجْعَلُ ٱلْمُتَّقِينَ كَٱلْفُجَّارِ (٢٨) كِتَٰبٌ أَنزَلْنَٰهُ إِلَيْكَ مُبَٰرَكٌ لِّيَدَّبَّرُوٓاْ ءَايَٰتِهِۦ وَلِيَتَذَكَّرَ أُوْلُواْ ٱلْأَلْبَٰبِ (٢٩)

Shall We treat those who believe (in the Oneness of Allâh − Islâmic Monotheism) and do righteous good deeds, as Mufsidûn (those who associate partners in worship with Allâh and commit crimes) on earth? Or shall We treat the Muttaqûn (pious), as the Fujjâr (criminals, disbelievers, the wicked)? (28) (This is) a Book (the Qur'ân) which We have sent down to you, full of blessings that they may ponder over its Verses, and that men of understanding may remember. (29)

Quran 39:17-19

وَٱلَّذِينَ ٱجْتَنَبُواْ ٱلطَّٰغُوتَ أَن يَعْبُدُوهَا وَأَنَابُوٓاْ إِلَى ٱللَّهِ لَهُمُ ٱلْبُشْرَىٰ فَبَشِّرْ عِبَادِ (١٧) ٱلَّذِينَ يَسْتَمِعُونَ ٱلْقَوْلَ فَيَتَّبِعُونَ أَحْسَنَهُۥٓ أُوْلَٰٓئِكَ ٱلَّذِينَ هَدَىٰهُمُ ٱللَّهُ وَأُوْلَٰٓئِكَ هُمْ أُوْلُواْ ٱلْأَلْبَٰبِ (١٨) أَفَمَنْ حَقَّ عَلَيْهِ كَلِمَةُ ٱلْعَذَابِ أَفَأَنتَ تُنقِذُ مَن فِى ٱلنَّارِ (١٩)

Those who avoid At-Tâghût (false deities) by not worshipping them and turn to Allâh (in repentance), for them are glad tidings; so announce the good news to My slaves, − (17) Those who listen to the Word [good advice Lâ ilâha ill-allâh − (none has the right to be worshipped but Allâh) and Islâmic Monotheism] and follow the best thereof (i.e. worship Allâh Alone, repent to Him and avoid Tâghût) those are (the ones) whom Allâh has guided and those are men of understanding. (18) Is, then one against whom the Word of punishment is justified (equal to the one who avoids evil)? Will you rescue him who is in the Fire? (19)

Quran 39:22-29

أَفَمَن شَرَحَ ٱللَّهُ صَدْرَهُۥ لِلْإِسْلَٰمِ فَهُوَ عَلَىٰ نُورٍ مِّن رَّبِّهِۦ فَوَيْلٌ لِّلْقَٰسِيَةِ قُلُوبُهُم مِّن ذِكْرِ ٱللَّهِ أُوْلَٰٓئِكَ فِى ضَلَٰلٍ مُّبِينٍ (٢٢) ٱللَّهُ نَزَّلَ أَحْسَنَ ٱلْحَدِيثِ كِتَٰبًا مُّتَشَٰبِهًا مَّثَانِىَ تَقْشَعِرُّ مِنْهُ جُلُودُ ٱلَّذِينَ يَخْشَوْنَ رَبَّهُمْ ثُمَّ تَلِينُ جُلُودُهُمْ وَقُلُوبُهُمْ إِلَىٰ ذِكْرِ ٱللَّهِ ذَٰلِكَ هُدَى ٱللَّهِ يَهْدِى بِهِۦ مَن يَشَآءُ وَمَن يُضْلِلِ ٱللَّهُ فَمَا لَهُۥ مِنْ هَادٍ (٢٣) أَفَمَن يَتَّقِى بِوَجْهِهِۦ سُوٓءَ ٱلْعَذَابِ يَوْمَ ٱلْقِيَٰمَةِ وَقِيلَ لِلظَّٰلِمِينَ ذُوقُواْ مَا كُنتُمْ تَكْسِبُونَ (٢٤) كَذَّبَ ٱلَّذِينَ مِن قَبْلِهِمْ

فَأَتَىٰهُمُ ٱلْعَذَابُ مِنْ حَيْثُ لَا يَشْعُرُونَ (٢٥) فَأَذَاقَهُمُ ٱللَّهُ ٱلْخِزْىَ فِى ٱلْحَيَوٰةِ ٱلدُّنْيَا ۖ
وَلَعَذَابُ ٱلْآخِرَةِ أَكْبَرُ ۚ لَوْ كَانُوا۟ يَعْلَمُونَ (٢٦) وَلَقَدْ ضَرَبْنَا لِلنَّاسِ فِى هَٰذَا ٱلْقُرْءَانِ مِن
كُلِّ مَثَلٍ لَّعَلَّهُمْ يَتَذَكَّرُونَ (٢٧) قُرْءَانًا عَرَبِيًّا غَيْرَ ذِى عِوَجٍ لَّعَلَّهُمْ يَتَّقُونَ
(٢٨) ضَرَبَ ٱللَّهُ مَثَلًا رَّجُلًا فِيهِ شُرَكَآءُ مُتَشَٰكِسُونَ وَرَجُلًا سَلَمًا لِّرَجُلٍ هَلْ يَسْتَوِيَانِ
مَثَلًا ۚ ٱلْحَمْدُ لِلَّهِ ۚ بَلْ أَكْثَرُهُمْ لَا يَعْلَمُونَ (٢٩)

Is he whose breast Allâh has opened to Islâm, so that he is in light from His Lord (as he who is non-Muslim)? So, woe to those whose hearts are hardened against remembrance of Allâh! They are in plain error! (22) Allâh has sent down the Best statement, a Book (this Qur'ân), its parts resembling each other (in goodness and truth), and oft-repeated. The skins of those who fear their Lord shiver from it (when they recite it or hear it). Then their skin and their heart soften to the remembrance of Allâh. That is the guidance of Allâh. He Guides therewith whom He wills and whomever Allâh sends astray, for him there is no guide. (23) Is he then, who will confront with his face the awful torment on the Day of Resurrection (as he who enters peacefully in Paradise)? And it will be said to the Zâlimûn (polytheists and wrong-doers): "Taste what you used to earn!" (24) Those before them belied, and so the torment came on them from directions they perceived not. (25) So Allâh made them to taste the disgrace in the present life, but greater is the torment of the Hereafter if they only knew! (26) And indeed We have put forth for men, in this Qur'ân every kind of similitude in order that they may remember. (27) An Arabic Qur'ân, without any crookedness (therein) in order that they may avoid all evil which Allâh has ordered them to avoid, fear Him and keep their duty to Him (28) Allâh puts forth a similitude: a (slave) man belonging to many partners (like those who worship others along with Allâh) disputing with one another, and a (slave) man belonging entirely to one master, (like those who worship Allâh Alone). Are those two equal in comparison? All the praises and thanks are to Allâh! But most of them know not. (29)

Quran 41:41-45

إِنَّ ٱلَّذِينَ كَفَرُوا۟ بِٱلذِّكْرِ لَمَّا جَآءَهُمْ ۖ وَإِنَّهُۥ لَكِتَٰبٌ عَزِيزٌ (٤١) لَّا يَأْتِيهِ ٱلْبَٰطِلُ مِنۢ بَيْنِ
يَدَيْهِ وَلَا مِنْ خَلْفِهِۦ ۖ تَنزِيلٌ مِّنْ حَكِيمٍ حَمِيدٍ (٤٢) مَّا يُقَالُ لَكَ إِلَّا مَا قَدْ قِيلَ لِلرُّسُلِ مِن

قَبْلِكَ إِنَّ رَبَّكَ لَذُو مَغْفِرَةٍ وَذُو عِقَابٍ أَلِيمٍ (٤٣) وَلَوْ جَعَلْنَاهُ قُرْءَانًا أَعْجَمِيًّا لَّقَالُوا۟ لَوْلَا فُصِّلَتْ ءَايَاتُهُۥٓ ۖ ءَا۬عْجَمِيٌّ وَعَرَبِيٌّ ۗ قُلْ هُوَ لِلَّذِينَ ءَامَنُوا۟ هُدًى وَشِفَآءٌ ۖ وَٱلَّذِينَ لَا يُؤْمِنُونَ فِىٓ ءَاذَانِهِمْ وَقْرٌ وَهُوَ عَلَيْهِمْ عَمًى ۚ أُو۟لَٰٓئِكَ يُنَادَوْنَ مِن مَّكَانٍۭ بَعِيدٍ (٤٤) وَلَقَدْ ءَاتَيْنَا مُوسَى ٱلْكِتَٰبَ فَٱخْتُلِفَ فِيهِ ۗ وَلَوْلَا كَلِمَةٌ سَبَقَتْ مِن رَّبِّكَ لَقُضِىَ بَيْنَهُمْ ۚ وَإِنَّهُمْ لَفِى شَكٍّ مِّنْهُ مُرِيبٍ (٤٥)

Verily, those who disbelieved in the Reminder (i.e. the Qur'ân) when it came to them (shall receive the punishment). And verily, it is an honourable well-fortified respected Book (because it is Allâh's Speech, and He has protected it from corruption). (See v.15:9) (41) Falsehood cannot come to it from before it or behind it (it is) sent down by the All-Wise, Worthy of all praise (Allâh). (42) Nothing is said to you (O Muhammad) except what was said to the Messengers before you. Verily, your Lord is the Possessor of forgiveness, and (also) the Possessor of painful punishment. (43) And if We had sent this as a Qur'ân in a foreign language (other than Arabic), they would have said: "Why are not its Verses explained in detail (in our language)? What! (A Book) not in Arabic and (the Messenger) an Arab?" Say: "It is for those who believe, a guide and a healing. And as for those who disbelieve, there is heaviness (deafness) in their ears, and it (the Qur'ân) is blindness for them. They are those who are called from a place far away (so they neither listen nor understand). (44) And indeed We gave Mûsa (Moses) the Scripture, but dispute arose therein. And had it not been for a Word that went forth before from your Lord, (the torment would have overtaken them) and the matter would have been settled between them. But truly, they are in grave doubt thereto (i.e. about the Qur'ân). (45)

Quran 42:15-17

فَلِذَٰلِكَ فَٱدْعُ ۖ وَٱسْتَقِمْ كَمَآ أُمِرْتَ ۖ وَلَا تَتَّبِعْ أَهْوَآءَهُمْ ۖ وَقُلْ ءَامَنتُ بِمَآ أَنزَلَ ٱللَّهُ مِن كِتَٰبٍ ۖ وَأُمِرْتُ لِأَعْدِلَ بَيْنَكُمُ ۖ ٱللَّهُ رَبُّنَا وَرَبُّكُمْ ۖ لَنَآ أَعْمَٰلُنَا وَلَكُمْ أَعْمَٰلُكُمْ ۖ لَا حُجَّةَ بَيْنَنَا وَبَيْنَكُمُ ۖ ٱللَّهُ يَجْمَعُ بَيْنَنَا ۖ وَإِلَيْهِ ٱلْمَصِيرُ (١٥) وَٱلَّذِينَ يُحَآجُّونَ فِى ٱللَّهِ مِنۢ بَعْدِ مَا ٱسْتُجِيبَ لَهُۥ حُجَّتُهُمْ دَاحِضَةٌ عِندَ رَبِّهِمْ وَعَلَيْهِمْ غَضَبٌ وَلَهُمْ عَذَابٌ شَدِيدٌ (١٦) ٱللَّهُ ٱلَّذِىٓ أَنزَلَ ٱلْكِتَٰبَ بِٱلْحَقِّ وَٱلْمِيزَانَ ۗ وَمَا يُدْرِيكَ لَعَلَّ ٱلسَّاعَةَ قَرِيبٌ (١٧)

So unto this (religion of Islâm alone and this Qur'ân) then invite (people) (O Muhammad), and stand firm [on Islâmic Monotheism by performing all that is ordained by Allâh (good deeds), and by abstaining from all that is forbidden by Allâh (sins and evil deeds)], as you are commanded, and follow not their desires but say: "I believe in whatsoever Allâh has sent down of the Book [all the holy Books, - this Qur'ân and the Books of the old from the Taurât (Torah), or the Injeel or the Pages of Ibrâhîm (Abraham)] and I am commanded to do justice among you. Allâh is our Lord and your Lord. For us our deeds and for you your deeds. There is no dispute between us and you. Allâh will assemble us (all), and to Him is the final return." (15) And those who dispute concerning Allâh (His religion of Islâmic Monotheism, with which Muhammad has been sent), after it has been accepted (by the people), of no use is their dispute before their Lord, and on them is wrath, and for them will be a severe torment. (16) It is Allâh Who has sent down the Book (the Qur'ân) in truth, and the Balance (i.e. to act justly). And what can make you know that perhaps the Hour is close at hand? (17)

Quran 43:78

لَقَدْ جِئْنَـٰكُم بِٱلْحَقِّ وَلَـٰكِنَّ أَكْثَرَكُمْ لِلْحَقِّ كَـٰرِهُونَ (٧٨)

Indeed We have brought the truth (Muhammad with the Qur'ân), to you, but most of you have a hatred for the truth. (78)

Quran 44:17-19

وَلَقَدْ فَتَنَّا قَبْلَهُمْ قَوْمَ فِرْعَوْنَ وَجَآءَهُمْ رَسُولٌ كَرِيمٌ (١٧) أَنْ أَدُّواْ إِلَىَّ عِبَادَ ٱللَّهِ إِنِّى لَكُمْ رَسُولٌ أَمِينٌ (١٨) وَأَن لَّا تَعْلُواْ عَلَى ٱللَّهِ إِنِّىٓ ءَاتِيكُم بِسُلْطَـٰنٍ مُّبِينٍ (١٩)

And indeed We tried before them Fir'aun's (Pharaoh) people, when there came to them a noble Messenger [i.e. Mûsa (Moses)], (17) Saying: "Deliver to me the slaves of Allâh (i.e. the Children of Israel). Verily! I am to you a Messenger worthy of all trust, (18) "And exalt not yourselves against Allâh. Truly, I have come to you with a manifest authority. (19)

Quran 44:32

وَلَقَدِ ٱخْتَرْنَـٰهُمْ عَلَىٰ عِلْمٍ عَلَى ٱلْعَـٰلَمِينَ (٣٢)

*And We chose them (the Children of Israel) above the 'Alamîn (mankind,
and jinn) [during the time of Mûsa (Moses)] with knowledge, (32)*

Quran 45:6-11

تِلْكَ ءَايَـٰتُ ٱللَّهِ نَتْلُوهَا عَلَيْكَ بِٱلْحَقِّ فَبِأَىِّ حَدِيثٍ بَعْدَ ٱللَّهِ وَءَايَـٰتِهِۦ يُؤْمِنُونَ (٦) وَيْلٌ
لِّكُلِّ أَفَّاكٍ أَثِيمٍ (٧) يَسْمَعُ ءَايَـٰتِ ٱللَّهِ تُتْلَىٰ عَلَيْهِ ثُمَّ يُصِرُّ مُسْتَكْبِرًا كَأَن لَّمْ يَسْمَعْهَا
فَبَشِّرْهُ بِعَذَابٍ أَلِيمٍ (٨) وَإِذَا عَلِمَ مِنْ ءَايَـٰتِنَا شَيْئًا ٱتَّخَذَهَا هُزُوًا أُوْلَـٰئِكَ لَهُمْ عَذَابٌ
مُّهِينٌ (٩) مِّن وَرَآئِهِمْ جَهَنَّمُ وَلَا يُغْنِى عَنْهُم مَّا كَسَبُواْ شَيْئًا وَلَا مَا ٱتَّخَذُواْ مِن دُونِ
ٱللَّهِ أَوْلِيَآءَ وَلَهُمْ عَذَابٌ عَظِيمٌ (١٠) هَـٰذَا هُدًى وَٱلَّذِينَ كَفَرُواْ بِـَٔايَـٰتِ رَبِّهِمْ لَهُمْ عَذَابٌ
مِّن رِّجْزٍ أَلِيمٌ (١١)

*These are the Ayât (proofs, evidences, verses, lessons, revelations, etc.) of
Allâh, which We recite to you (O Muhammad) with truth. Then in which
speech after Allâh and His Ayât will they believe? (6) Woe to every sinful
liar, (7) Who hears the Verses of Allâh (being) recited to him, yet persists
with pride as if he heard them not. So announce to him a painful torment!
(8) And when he learns something of Our Verses (this Qur'ân), he makes
them a jest. For such there will be a humiliating torment. (9) In front of
them there is Hell, and that which they have earned will be of no profit to
them, nor (will be of any profit to them) those whom they have taken as
Auliyâ' (protectors, helpers) besides Allâh. And theirs will be a great
torment. (10) This (Qur'ân) is a guidance. And those who disbelieve in
the Ayât (proofs, evidences, verses, lessons, signs, revelations) of their
Lord, for them there is a painful torment of Rijz (a severe kind of
punishment). (11)*

Quran 45:16-21

وَلَقَدْ ءَاتَيْنَا بَنِى إِسْرَآءِيلَ ٱلْكِتَـٰبَ وَٱلْحُكْمَ وَٱلنُّبُوَّةَ وَرَزَقْنَـٰهُم مِّنَ ٱلطَّيِّبَـٰتِ وَفَضَّلْنَـٰهُمْ
عَلَى ٱلْعَـٰلَمِينَ (١٦) وَءَاتَيْنَـٰهُم بَيِّنَـٰتٍ مِّنَ ٱلْأَمْرِ فَمَا ٱخْتَلَفُوٓاْ إِلَّا مِنۢ بَعْدِ مَا جَآءَهُمُ
ٱلْعِلْمُ بَغْيًۢا بَيْنَهُمْ إِنَّ رَبَّكَ يَقْضِى بَيْنَهُمْ يَوْمَ ٱلْقِيَـٰمَةِ فِيمَا كَانُواْ فِيهِ يَخْتَلِفُونَ (١٧) ثُمَّ
جَعَلْنَـٰكَ عَلَىٰ شَرِيعَةٍ مِّنَ ٱلْأَمْرِ فَٱتَّبِعْهَا وَلَا تَتَّبِعْ أَهْوَآءَ ٱلَّذِينَ لَا يَعْلَمُونَ (١٨) إِنَّهُمْ لَن
يُغْنُواْ عَنكَ مِنَ ٱللَّهِ شَيْئًا وَإِنَّ ٱلظَّـٰلِمِينَ بَعْضُهُمْ أَوْلِيَآءُ بَعْضٍ وَٱللَّهُ وَلِىُّ ٱلْمُتَّقِينَ

(١٩) هَٰذَا بَصَٰئِرُ لِلنَّاسِ وَهُدًى وَرَحْمَةٌ لِّقَوْمٍ يُوقِنُونَ (٢٠) أَمْ حَسِبَ ٱلَّذِينَ ٱجْتَرَحُواْ ٱلسَّيِّئَاتِ أَن نَّجْعَلَهُمْ كَٱلَّذِينَ ءَامَنُواْ وَعَمِلُواْ ٱلصَّٰلِحَٰتِ سَوَآءً مَّحْيَاهُمْ وَمَمَاتُهُمْ سَآءَ مَا يَحْكُمُونَ (٢١)

And indeed We gave the Children of Israel the Scripture, and the understanding of the Scripture and its laws, and the Prophethood; and provided them with good things, and preferred them above the 'Alamîn (mankind and jinn of their time, during that period), (16) And gave them clear proofs in matters [by revealing to them the Taurât (Torah)]. And they differed not until after the knowledge came to them, through envy among themselves. Verily, Your Lord will judge between them on the Day of Resurrection about that wherein they used to differ. (17) Then We have put you (O Muhammad) on a (plain) way of (Our) commandment [like the one which We commanded Our Messengers before you (i.e. legal ways and laws of the Islâmic Monotheism)]. So follow you that (Islâmic Monotheism and its laws), and follow not the desires of those who know not. (Tafsir At-Tabarî) (18) Verily, they can avail you nothing against Allâh (if He wants to punish you). Verily, the Zâlimûn (polytheists, wrong-doers) are Auliyâ' (protectors, helpers) of one another, but Allâh is the Walî (Helper, Protector) of the Muttaqûn (pious). (19) This (Qur'ân) is a clear insight and evidence for mankind, and a guidance and a mercy for people who have Faith with certainty. (20) Or do those who earn evil deeds think that We shall hold them equal with those who believe (in the Oneness of Allâh — Islâmic Monotheism) and do righteous good deeds, in their present life and after their death? Worst is the judgement that they make. (21)

Quran 46:12

وَمِن قَبْلِهِ كِتَٰبُ مُوسَىٰٓ إِمَامًا وَرَحْمَةً وَهَٰذَا كِتَٰبٌ مُّصَدِّقٌ لِّسَانًا عَرَبِيًّا لِّيُنذِرَ ٱلَّذِينَ ظَلَمُواْ وَبُشْرَىٰ لِلْمُحْسِنِينَ (١٢)

And before this was the Scripture of Mûsâ (Moses) as a guide and a mercy. And this is a confirming Book (the Qur'ân) in the Arabic language, to warn those who do wrong, and as glad tidings to the Muhsinûn (good-doers.). (12)

Quran 47:14

أَفَمَن كَانَ عَلَىٰ بَيِّنَةٍ مِّن رَّبِّهِ كَمَن زُيِّنَ لَهُ سُوءُ عَمَلِهِ وَٱتَّبَعُوٓاْ أَهْوَآءَهُم (١٤)

Is he who is on a clear proof from his Lord, like those for whom their evil deeds that they do are beautified for them, while they follow their own lusts (evil desires)? (14)

Quran 48:28

هُوَ ٱلَّذِىٓ أَرْسَلَ رَسُولَهُ بِٱلْهُدَىٰ وَدِينِ ٱلْحَقِّ لِيُظْهِرَهُ عَلَى ٱلدِّينِ كُلِّهِ وَكَفَىٰ بِٱللَّهِ شَهِيدًا (٢٨)

He it is Who has sent His Messenger (Muhammad) with guidance and the religion of truth (Islâm), that He may make it (Islâm) superior over all religions. And All-Sufficient is Allâh as a Witness. (28)

Quran 49:7-8

وَٱعْلَمُوٓاْ أَنَّ فِيكُمْ رَسُولَ ٱللَّهِ لَوْ يُطِيعُكُمْ فِى كَثِيرٍ مِّنَ ٱلْأَمْرِ لَعَنِتُّمْ وَلَٰكِنَّ ٱللَّهَ حَبَّبَ إِلَيْكُمُ ٱلْإِيمَٰنَ وَزَيَّنَهُ فِى قُلُوبِكُمْ وَكَرَّهَ إِلَيْكُمُ ٱلْكُفْرَ وَٱلْفُسُوقَ وَٱلْعِصْيَانَ أُوْلَٰٓئِكَ هُمُ ٱلرَّٰشِدُونَ (٧) فَضْلاً مِّنَ ٱللَّهِ وَنِعْمَةً وَٱللَّهُ عَلِيمٌ حَكِيمٌ (٨)

And know that, among you there is the Messenger of Allâh. If he were to obey you (i.e. follow your opinions and desires) in much of the matter, you would surely be in trouble, But Allâh has endeared the Faith to you and has beautified it in your hearts, and has made disbelief, wickedness and disobedience (to Allâh and His Messenger) hateful to you. Such are they who are the rightly guided, (7) (This is) a Grace from Allâh and His Favour. And Allâh is All-Knowing, All-Wise. (8)

Quran 53:2-6

مَا ضَلَّ صَاحِبُكُمْ وَمَا غَوَىٰ (٢) وَمَا يَنطِقُ عَنِ ٱلْهَوَىٰ (٣) إِنْ هُوَ إِلَّا وَحْىٌ يُوحَىٰ (٤) عَلَّمَهُ شَدِيدُ ٱلْقُوَىٰ (٥) ذُو مِرَّةٍ فَٱسْتَوَىٰ (٦)

Your companion (Muhammad) has neither gone astray nor has erred. (2) Nor does he speak of (his own) desire. (3) It is only a Revelation revealed. (4) He has been taught (this Qur'ân) by one mighty in power

[Jibril (Gabriel)] (5) One free from any defect in body and mind, then he (Jibril — Gabriel in the real shap as created by Allah) rose and became stable. (6)

Quran 53:24

أَمْ لِلْإِنسَٰنِ مَا تَمَنَّىٰ (٢٤)

Or shall man have what he wishes? (24)

Quran 56:75-81

فَلَآ أُقْسِمُ بِمَوَٰقِعِ ٱلنُّجُومِ (٧٥) وَإِنَّهُۥ لَقَسَمٌ لَّوْ تَعْلَمُونَ عَظِيمٌ (٧٦) إِنَّهُۥ لَقُرْءَانٌ كَرِيمٌ (٧٧) فِى كِتَٰبٍ مَّكْنُونٍ (٧٨) لَّا يَمَسُّهُۥٓ إِلَّا ٱلْمُطَهَّرُونَ (٧٩) تَنزِيلٌ مِّن رَّبِّ ٱلْعَٰلَمِينَ (٨٠) أَفَبِهَٰذَا ٱلْحَدِيثِ أَنتُم مُّدْهِنُونَ (٨١)

So I swear by the setting of the stars. (75) And verily, that is indeed a great oath, if you but know. (76) That (this) is indeed an honourable recitation (the Noble Qur'ân). (77) In a Book well-guarded (with Allâh in the heaven i.e. Al-Lauh Al-Mahfûz). (78) Which (that Book with Allâh) none can touch but the purified (i.e. the angels). (79) A Revelation (this Qur'ân) from the Lord of the 'Alamîn (mankind, jinn and all that exists). (80) Is it such a talk (this Qur'an) that you (disbelievers) deny? (81)

Quran 58:5

إِنَّ ٱلَّذِينَ يُحَآدُّونَ ٱللَّهَ وَرَسُولَهُۥ كُبِتُوا۟ كَمَا كُبِتَ ٱلَّذِينَ مِن قَبْلِهِمْ وَقَدْ أَنزَلْنَآ ءَايَٰتٍۭ بَيِّنَٰتٍ وَلِلْكَٰفِرِينَ عَذَابٌ مُّهِينٌ (٥)

Verily, those who oppose Allâh and His Messenger (Muhammad) will be disgraced, as those before them (among the past nation), were disgraced. And We have sent down clear Ayât (proofs, evidences, verses, lessons, signs, revelations, etc.). And for the disbelievers is a disgracing torment. (5)

Quran 58:20-22

إِنَّ ٱلَّذِينَ يُحَآدُّونَ ٱللَّهَ وَرَسُولَهُۥٓ أُو۟لَٰٓئِكَ فِى ٱلْأَذَلِّينَ (٢٠) كَتَبَ ٱللَّهُ لَأَغْلِبَنَّ أَنَا۠ وَرُسُلِىٓ إِنَّ ٱللَّهَ قَوِىٌّ عَزِيزٌ (٢١) لَّا تَجِدُ قَوْمًا يُؤْمِنُونَ بِٱللَّهِ وَٱلْيَوْمِ ٱلْءَاخِرِ يُوَآدُّونَ مَنْ

حَادَّ ٱللَّهَ وَرَسُولَهُ ۚ وَلَوْ كَانُوٓاْ ءَابَآءَهُمْ أَوْ أَبْنَآءَهُمْ أَوْ إِخْوَٰنَهُمْ أَوْ عَشِيرَتَهُمْ ۚ أُوْلَٰٓئِكَ كَتَبَ فِى قُلُوبِهِمُ ٱلْإِيمَٰنَ وَأَيَّدَهُم بِرُوحٍ مِّنْهُ ۖ وَيُدْخِلُهُمْ جَنَّٰتٍ تَجْرِى مِن تَحْتِهَا ٱلْأَنْهَٰرُ خَٰلِدِينَ فِيهَا ۚ رَضِىَ ٱللَّهُ عَنْهُمْ وَرَضُواْ عَنْهُ ۚ أُوْلَٰٓئِكَ حِزْبُ ٱللَّهِ ۚ أَلَآ إِنَّ حِزْبَ ٱللَّهِ هُمُ ٱلْمُفْلِحُونَ (٢٢)

Those who oppose Allâh and His Messenger (Muhammad), they will be among the lowest (most humiliated). (20) Allâh has decreed: "Verily! It is I and My Messengers who shall be the victorious." Verily, Allâh is All-Powerful, All-Mighty. (21) You (O Muhammad) will not find any people who believe in Allâh and the Last Day, making friendship with those who oppose Allâh and His Messenger (Muhammad), even though they were their fathers or their sons or their brothers or their kindred (people). For such He has written Faith in their hearts, and strengthened them with Rûh (proofs, light and true guidance) from Himself. And He will admit them to Gardens (Paradise) under which rivers flow to dwell therein (forever). Allâh is pleased with them, and they with Him. They are the Party of Allâh. Verily, it is the Party of Allâh that will be the successful. (22)

Quran 59:20

لَا يَسْتَوِىٓ أَصْحَٰبُ ٱلنَّارِ وَأَصْحَٰبُ ٱلْجَنَّةِ ۚ أَصْحَٰبُ ٱلْجَنَّةِ هُمُ ٱلْفَآئِزُونَ (٢٠)

Not equal are the dwellers of the Fire and the dwellers of the Paradise. It is the dwellers of Paradise that will be successful. (20)

Quran 61:9

هُوَ ٱلَّذِىٓ أَرْسَلَ رَسُولَهُ بِٱلْهُدَىٰ وَدِينِ ٱلْحَقِّ لِيُظْهِرَهُ ۥ عَلَى ٱلدِّينِ كُلِّهِۦ وَلَوْ كَرِهَ ٱلْمُشْرِكُونَ (٩)

He it is Who has sent His Messenger (Muhammad) with guidance and the religion of truth (Islâmic Monotheism) to make it victorious over all (other) religions even though the Mushrikûn (polytheists, pagans, idolaters, and disbelievers in the Oneness of Allâh and in His Messenger Muhammed) hate (it). (9)

Quran 62:2-5

هُوَ ٱلَّذِى بَعَثَ فِى ٱلْأُمِّيِّنَ رَسُولاً مِّنْهُمْ يَتْلُواْ عَلَيْهِمْ ءَايَٰتِهِۦ وَيُزَكِّيهِمْ وَيُعَلِّمُهُمُ ٱلْكِتَٰبَ وَٱلْحِكْمَةَ وَإِن كَانُواْ مِن قَبْلُ لَفِى ضَلَٰلٍ مُّبِينٍ (٢) وَءَاخَرِينَ مِنْهُمْ لَمَّا يَلْحَقُواْ بِهِمْ وَهُوَ ٱلْعَزِيزُ ٱلْحَكِيمُ (٣) ذَٰلِكَ فَضْلُ ٱللَّهِ يُؤْتِيهِ مَن يَشَآءُ وَٱللَّهُ ذُو ٱلْفَضْلِ ٱلْعَظِيمِ (٤) مَثَلُ ٱلَّذِينَ حُمِّلُواْ ٱلتَّوْرَٰةَ ثُمَّ لَمْ يَحْمِلُوهَا كَمَثَلِ ٱلْحِمَارِ يَحْمِلُ أَسْفَارًا بِئْسَ مَثَلُ ٱلْقَوْمِ ٱلَّذِينَ كَذَّبُواْ بِـَٔايَٰتِ ٱللَّهِ وَٱللَّهُ لَا يَهْدِى ٱلْقَوْمَ ٱلظَّٰلِمِينَ (٥)

He it is Who sent among the unlettered ones a Messenger (Muhammad) from among themselves, reciting to them His Verses, purifying them (from the filth of disbelief and polytheism), and teaching them the Book (this Qur'ân, Islâmic laws and Islâmic jurisprudence) and Al-Hikmah (As-Sunnah: legal ways, orders, acts of worship, of Prophet Muhammad). And verily, they had been before in mainfest error; (2) And [He has sent him (Prophet Muhammad) also to] others among them (Muslims) who have not yet joined them (but they will come). And He (Allâh) is the All-Mighty, the All-Wise. (3) That is the Grace of Allâh, which He bestows on whom He wills. And Allâh is the Owner of Mighty Grace. (4) The likeness of those who were entrusted with the (obligation of the) Taurât (Torah) (i.e. to obey its commandments and to practise its laws), but who subsequently failed in those (obligations), is as the likeness of a donkey which carries huge burdens of books (but understands nothing from them). How bad is the example of people who deny the Ayât (proofs, evidences, verses, signs, revelations) of Allâh. And Allâh guides not the people who are Zâlimûn (polytheists, wrong-doers, disbelievers). (5)

Quran 68:35-40

أَفَنَجْعَلُ ٱلْمُسْلِمِينَ كَٱلْمُجْرِمِينَ (٣٥) مَا لَكُمْ كَيْفَ تَحْكُمُونَ (٣٦) أَمْ لَكُمْ كِتَٰبٌ فِيهِ تَدْرُسُونَ (٣٧) إِنَّ لَكُمْ فِيهِ لَمَا تَخَيَّرُونَ (٣٨) أَمْ لَكُمْ أَيْمَٰنٌ عَلَيْنَا بَٰلِغَةٌ إِلَىٰ يَوْمِ ٱلْقِيَٰمَةِ إِنَّ لَكُمْ لَمَا تَحْكُمُونَ (٣٩) سَلْهُمْ أَيُّهُم بِذَٰلِكَ زَعِيمٌ (٤٠)

Shall We then treat the Muslims (believers of Islamic Monotheism, doers of righteous deeds) like the Mujrimûn (criminals, polytheists and disbelievers)? (35) What is the matter with you? How judge you? (36) Or have you a Book where in you learn, (37) That you shall therein have all that you choose? (38) Or have you oaths from Us, reaching to the Day of

Resurrection that yours will be what you judge? (39) Ask them, which of them will stand surety for that! (40)

I will end with some advice from Muhammad the Messenger of Allah, peace be upon him and all the prophets of Allah, who we pledge allegiance to.

Abu Sa'id al-Khudri reported: The Messenger of Allah, peace and blessings be upon him, said:

Whoever among you sees evil, let him change it with his hand. If he is unable to do so, then with his tongue. If he is unable to do so, then with his heart, and that is the weakest level of faith.

Source: Ṣaḥīḥ Muslim 49

Hudhayfah ibn al-Yaman reported: The people used to ask the Messenger of Allah, peace and blessings be upon him, about good, but I would ask about evil for fear it would overtake me. I said, "O Messenger of Allah, we were in ignorance and evil and Allah sent us this good. Will there be evil after this good?" The Prophet said, "**Yes.**" I said, "Will there be good after that evil?" The Prophet said, "**Yes, but within it is smoke.**" I said, "What is its smoke?" The Prophet said, "**A people who are not guided by my guidance. You will recognize them and reject them.**" I said, "Will there be evil after that good?" The Prophet said, "**Yes, callers to the gates of Hellfire. Whoever answers them will taste it from within.**" I said, "O Messenger of Allah, describe them to us." The Prophet said, "They are from our progeny and speak our language." I said, "What do you command me should that overtake me?" The Prophet said, "**Hold fast to the community of Muslims and their leader.**" I said, "What if there is no community and no leader?" The Prophet said, "**Then withdraw from all of the sects, even if you must bite at the root of trees until death overtakes you in that state.**"

Source: Ṣaḥīḥ al-Bukhārī 3606, Ṣaḥīḥ Muslim 1847

www.ingramcontent.com/pod-product-compliance
Lightning Source LLC
Chambersburg PA
CBHW060240030426
42335CB00014B/1542